DGAAM

Study Guide

Alastair Younger
University of Ottowa

Child Psychology
Fourth Edition

Ross Vasta
State University of New York at Brockport

Scott A. Miller
University of Florida

Shari Ellis
University of Florida

WILEY

JOHN WILEY & SONS, INC.

Cover Photo: ©Elyse Lewin/The Image Bank/Getty Images

To order books or for customer service call 1-800-CALL-WILEY (225-5945).

ISBN 0-471-65048-X

Printed in the United States of America

10 9 8 7 6 5 4 3 2 1

Printed and bound Courier – Kendallville, Inc.

Contents

Preface
How to Use This Study Guide

Congratulations on having purchased the study guide to accompany **Child Psychology: The Modern Science** *(4th edition)*. The purpose of the study guide is to get you actively involved in learning the material in your textbook. Its goal is to help you better learn, understand, and apply the concepts from the textbook. Proper use of the study guide, therefore, will enhance your learning of the material.

The study guide has been designed to facilitate *active* learning. For many students, studying is a passive process. They attend class, read the material, and so on, but in each of these activities they serve as relatively passive targets to whom material is presented. Even when they study, they remain relatively passive -- they re-read the text or passages they have highlighted, copy their notes, and so on. Although these strategies are part of studying, they do not involve actively testing your knowledge of the material. By contrast, active learning demands that you take control of the learning process by continually testing your knowledge. This study guide incorporates a variety of techniques that will enable you to evaluate what you have learned and to "zero in" on areas in which your knowledge and/or understanding fall short. The following paragraphs outline specific suggestions concerning how to use the study guide to your best advantage.

Read and Study the Chapter

The first step in using the study guide is to read the chapter in the text carefully. Only after carefully reading the chapter are you ready to use the study guide to help you actively learn the material and to evaluate your learning. Read through each chapter and highlight the most important parts. Pay particular attention to the key terms that are used and the key concepts that are discussed. Once you have read through the chapter, you may then begin using the study guide to assist you in learning and understanding the material in the chapter.

Work Through the Study Guide

The next step is to work through the study guide. Each chapter of the study guide includes the following tools designed to help you actively learn the material: OUTLINE, LEARNING OBJECTIVES, KEY TERMS, FILL-IN EXERCISES, APPLICATION, USING WHAT YOU HAVE LEARNED, SAMPLE TEST QUESTIONS, and ANSWERS.

Outline

Each chapter begins with an outline. This will be your starting point. The outline is an overview of the contents of the chapter. After carefully reading the chapter, enter your questions, comments, and notes in the space under each topic in the outline. Write down terms or concepts you don't understand with their page numbers and re-read these areas in the chapter.

Learning Objectives

Each chapter contains a list of learning objectives. These objectives are more specific than the topics listed in the outline. After reading the chapter, check off the learning objectives you are confident that you know. Review the material in the textbook for those about which you are less confident, recording the important points from your reading in the space below each objective.

Key Terms

Each chapter contains a list of key terms from the textbook. The key terms provide another way of assessing your knowledge of the material in the chapter. After carefully reading the chapter and completing the learning objectives, go through the list of key terms, one by one, and try to define each. Note each term that you feel uncertain of; this will indicate an area in the textbook that you need to review. After defining the key terms, you should then check that your definitions are correct. Go through the chapter and find the terms you have defined. Key terms that you are unsure of indicate areas of the text that you need to study further.

Fill-in Exercises

Fill-in exercises are another way to test your knowledge of the material in the chapter. These are a series of fill-in-the-blank sentences directly related to material from the chapter in the text. Go through these exercises, filling in the word or words that complete each sentence. Check your answers with those at the end of each chapter in the study guide. If you have a good understanding of the material, you should have a good idea of what words complete each sentence in the fill-in exercises. If you could not think of the word to complete a particular sentence, or it is not clear to you why the answer given is correct, this indicates a topic in the text that should be re-read. These exercises are more specific, and sometimes more "picky" than the previous exercises. They are a way to test your knowledge of specific facts in each chapter. They don't cover every possible fact, but sample from all topics in the chapter.

Using What You Have Learned and Application

These two sections consist of exercises that test your understanding of the material in the chapter by having you apply your knowledge. In most cases, you will be asked to apply what you have read from the chapter to a situation that is described to you. You may choose to work with other students on these exercises, or you may complete them alone. If you have a good understanding of the material in the chapter, you should be able to apply it to the situations described in these sections.

Sample Test Questions

Once you are confident that you have mastered the material in the chapter, you are then ready to try the sample test questions. These questions give you the chance to try out a practice multiple-choice test for the information in each chapter. As with any exam, read each question and answer thoroughly before attempting to choose the most correct answer. After completing the sample test questions, check your answers against those provided at the end of the chapter in the study guide.

If you answer a question incorrectly, it is important to ask the question "Why?" Sometimes people find that they knew the correct answer, but gave an incorrect answer because they didn't read the question carefully, didn't read through all the answers carefully before making their choice, or were just careless and marked the wrong answer. If any of these applies to you, then you have learned something about yourself that will be important to keep in mind when you take a real test -- read the question carefully, read all the answers carefully, and check that you mark your choice carefully. On the other hand, if you find that you did not know the correct answer, look up the topic in the textbook and review it. Remember, the purpose of the sample test is not just to get the right answer, but to *know* the right answer and to understand why it is correct. To accomplish this, you must attain a thorough understanding of the entire theory, concept, or information that gave you trouble. Make sure that in addition to understanding why a particular response was the *best* answer, you also understand why the other responses were *not*. This will help you gain a deeper understanding of both the main points and the subtleties of the material in the chapter. This is also a good tactic to apply when taking real multiple choice exams. Not only should you look for the best answer, but you should try to be sure that any other answers are *not* the best.

Answers

Finally, you will find the correct answers for the "Fill-in Exercises," the "Sample Test Questions," and occasionally for "Application" and "Using What You Have Learned" exercises. Check your answers against these, and go back and review those portions of the chapter where your answers were incorrect or where you did not know how to answer.

It would be a mistake to think that using the study guide could in any way *replace* reading the textbook. If this was your intention, I strongly advise you to reconsider. Simply looking at a couple of chapters in the study guide will show you that it was not designed to replace the textbook; it was designed to work hand-in-hand with the textbook to facilitate learning. Proper use of the study guide involves carefully reading each chapter in the textbook. In addition, to do well in your course, you must attend all classes and take good notes. In many classes, professors cover topics that may not be included in the text, or may elaborate on material that is in the text. Thus, even the most careful reading of the text cannot replace attending all classes and taking careful notes.

These are my suggestions for how to use your study guide to its best advantage. Good luck in your course! Most of all, ENJOY LEARNING ABOUT CHILD PSYCHOLOGY!

Chapter 1
Background and Theories

OUTLINE

Use this outline as you read the chapter. Enter your questions, comments, and notes in the space provided. Write down terms or statements you don't understand, with their page numbers.

DEVELOPMENTAL PSYCHOLOGY AND ITS ROOTS

What is Developmental Psychology?

Why Study Children?

Early Theorists

Pioneers of Child Psychology

ISSUES IN DEVELOPMENTAL PSYCHOLOGY

Nature versus Nurture

Continuity versus Discontinuity

Normative versus Idiographic Development

THEORIES OF DEVELOPMENT: COGNITIVE-DEVELOPMENTAL MODELS

Piaget's Theory

Information-Processing Models

THEORIES OF DEVELOPMENT: THE SOCIOCULTURAL APPROACH

Vygotsky's Theory

Bronfenbrenner's Ecological Model

THEORIES OF DEVELOPMENT: ENVIRONMENTAL/LEARNING APPROACHES

Defining Learning

B. F. Skinner

Types of Learning

Classics of Research
Little Albert and Little Peter

Social-Learning Theory

THEORIES OF DEVELOPMENT: EVOLUTIONARY AND BIOLOGICAL APPROACHES

Behavior and Evolution

Classical Ethology

Applications to Human Development

LEARNING OBJECTIVES

Upon completion of Chapter 1, you should be able to discuss the following topics. Check off those you are confident that you can discuss well. Re-read the material in the text for the topics about which you are less confident. Record the important points from your reading in the space below each topic.

1   Briefly discuss the views of childhood held during the ancient Greek and Roman period, the middle ages, and Renaissance period.

2.   Outline five reasons why developmental psychologists have concentrated their research on humans during the childhood years.

3.   Discuss the major theoretical assumptions of John Locke, Jean-Jacques Rousseau, Johann Gottried von Herder, and Charles Darwin.

4.   Explain how John Locke viewed the mind of the newborn and how Rousseau held a contrasting view.

5.   Describe the importance of language in Herder's view of development.

6.   Define the principle of *recapitulation,* which developed from Darwin's theory.

7.   Describe the contributions made to developmental psychology by G. Stanley Hall.

8.   Describe John B. Watson's view of how learning takes place.

9.   Discuss Arnold Gesell's views on the relative contributions of heredity and environment to development.

10.   Describe the five stages of development outlined in Freud's psychosexual model.

11.   Explain how Erikson's model of development differs from that of Freud.

12.　　Define and explain the following issues in developmental psychology:

　　　Nature versus Nurture

　　　Continuity versus Discontinuity

　　　Normative versus Idiographic Research

13.　　Explain how Piaget conceptualized intelligence.

14.　　Compare the processes of assimilation and accommodation and describe how they work together, according to Piaget's theory.

15.　　Contrast children's thinking during the sensorimotor, preoperational, concrete operations, and formal operations periods.

16.　　Explain how information-processing theorists conceptualize cognition as a three-part system.

17.　　Compare Vygotsky's sociocultural theory of cognitive development with Piaget's position, focusing particularly on the role of the environment.

18.　　Explain why Vygotsky's model of development has been termed a sociocultural approach.

19.　　Specify the conditions needed in order to infer that learning has taken place.

20.   How can Habituation and Dishabituation be considered forms of learning?

21.   Distinguish between respondent and operant conditioning.

22.   Explain how behaviors are learned and unlearned according to the *classical conditioning* approach.

23.   Distinguish between positive and negative reinforcement, and explain how these differ from punishment.

24.   Specify the four processes that Bandura believes underlie observational learning.

25.   Explain how the person, behavior, and environment interact in Bandura's social-cognitive account of learning.

26.   Specify the four qualities that characterize virtually all innate behaviors, according to ethologists.

27.   Explain what ethologists mean by the term *sensitive period*, using the phenomenon of imprinting as an example.

28.   Explain the basic notions of Bowlby's work and of sociobiology.

29.   Describe two major themes of evolutionary developmental psychology.

KEY TERMS

Upon completion of Chapter 1, you should be able to define the following terms.

Developmental psychology _____

_____

Tabula rasa _____

_____

Cultural relativism _____

_____

Nativism _____

_____

Natural selection _____

_____

Recapitulation _____

_____

Baby biography _____

_____

Zeitgeist _____

_____

Behaviorism _____

_____

Maturation _____

_____

Norms _____

_____

Repression _____

_____

Identification _____

_____

Interactionist perspective _____

_____

Identity _____

_____

Nature versus nurture debate _____

_____

Continuity versus discontinuity debate _____

_____

Normative versus idiographic development _____

_____

Universals of development _____

_____

Genetic epistemology _____

_____

Clinical method _____

_____

Schemes _____

_____

Organization _____

_____

Adaptation _____

_____

Assimilation _____

_____

Accommodation _____

_____

Constructivism _____

_____

Periods _____

_____

Sensorimotor _____

_____

Preoperational _____

_____

Concrete operations _____

_____

Formal operations   _____

_____

Tools of intellectual adaptation   _____

_____

Dialectical process   _____

_____

Internalization   _____

_____

Ecological perspective   _____

_____

Transactional influence   _____

_____

Microsystem   _____

_____

Mesosystem   _____

_____

Exosystem   _____

_____

Macrosystem   _____

_____

Chronosystem   _____

_____

Learning _____

_____

Reflex _____

_____

Respondent behavior _____

_____

Operant behavior _____

_____

Habituation _____

_____

Dishabituation _____

_____

Classical (respondent) conditioning _____

_____

Unconditioned stimulus (UCS) _____

_____

Unconditioned response (UCR) _____

_____

Conditioned stimulus (CS) _____

_____

Stimulus generalization _____

_____

Extinction _____

_____

Operant learning _____

_____

Positive reinforcer _____

_____

Negative reinforcer _____

_____

Punisher _____

_____

Social-learning theory _____

_____

Observational learning _____

_____

Vicarious reinforcement _____

_____

Vicarious punishment _____

_____

Imitation _____

_____

Response inhibition _____

_____

Reciprocal determinism _____

_____

Ethology _____

_____

Modal action pattern _____

_____

Innate releasing mechanism _____

_____

Imprinting _____

_____

Sensitive period _____

_____

Sociobiology _____

_____

Evolutionary developmental psychology _____

_____

FILL-IN EXERCISES

Fill in the word or words that best fit in the spaces below.

1. According to John Locke, the mind of the newborn is like a _____ _____.

2. The emphasis on inborn processes rather than environmental factors as the driving force in human development is referred to as _____.

3. The notion that development of the individual parallels the development of the species is referred to as the principle of _____.

4. The term _____, which literally means "the spirit of the times," refers to a theoretical idea that is generally shared by the scientists of a given period.

5. Gesell established statistical _____, or developmental timetables, describing the usual order in which children display various early behaviors and the age-range within which each behavior usually appears.

6. According to Freud, each child is born with a certain amount of sexual energy called _____, that is biologically guided to certain locations of the body called the _____ _____.

7. "Emergent abilities versus acquired skills" is another label for the issue of _____ versus _____.

8. The issue of _____ versus _____ has two components -- one concerns the pattern of development; the other concerns the connectedness of development.

9. _____ research is concerned with identifying commonalities in human development, whereas _____ research is concerned with differences in development from one child to the next.

10. Piaget described his own area of interest as _____ _____, or the study of the nature of knowledge in children.

11. A loosely structured interview format, employed by Piaget, in which he asked whatever questions or pursued whatever issues he felt would reveal the child's way of reasoning is referred to as the _____ _____.

12. Piaget described intelligence not as something a child *has*, but something a child _____.

13. A _____ consists of set of skilled, flexible action patterns through which the child understands the world.

14. Changing existing cognitive structures to fit with new experiences is called _____.

15. Attempting to fit a new experience into existing knowledge is called _____.

16. During the _____ period, the child begins to use symbols, such as words and numbers, to represent the world cognitively.

17. During the period of _____ operations, children are able to perform mental operations on the pieces of knowledge they possess.

18. Information-processing theorists view children's cognition as a system composed of _____ parts, which many feel is similar to the operation of a _____.

19.   Vygotsky believed that cognitive development results from a _____ process, in which the child learns through shared problem-solving experiences with someone else, usually a parent or teacher.

20.   Vygotsky used the term _____ to refer to the child's incorporation, largely through language, of bodies of knowledge and tools of thought from the culture.

21.   In Bronfenbrenner's ecological perspective, the system nearest the child, which includes the family, the school, the playground, and so forth is referred to as the _____. Social settings that can affect the child, but in which the child does not participate directly are referred to as the _____.

22.   Mr. Smith's class has just been shown how to multiply fractions. In order to establish that a pupil has learned this skill, a relatively _____ change in _____ must be demonstrated.

23.   _____ behaviors are controlled by their effects while _____ behaviors are controlled by the stimuli that elicit them.

24.   A young child is accidentally hit by a baseball. He develops a fear of baseball bats, caps, and gloves. This phenomenon is called _____ _____.

25.   As a consequence for her good behavior, Maria's parents let her watch TV for an extra ½ hour before bed. This consequence is referred to as _____ _____. Jorge, on the other hand, has had his TV time cut as a consequence for not doing his chores. This consequence is referred to as _____.

26.   Children are more likely to imitate a model they have observed if they see that the model has been _____.

27.   Bandura's model of *reciprocal determinism* depicts three influences which affect each other: characteristics of the _____, the _____, and the person's _____.

28.   Bowlby maintained that if _____ and _____ do not form a close emotional bond during the child's infancy (which is therefore a _____ period), the child may have difficulty forming close interpersonal relationships later on.

USING WHAT YOU HAVE LEARNED

A number of important figures in the history of developmental psychology were discussed in this chapter. Match the following historical individuals with the concept with which each is most closely associated.

Concepts	Figures
1. Tabula rasa	John Locke
2. Behaviorism	Jean-Jacques Rousseau
3. Repression	Johann Gottried von Herder
4. Norms	Charles Darwin
5. Identity	John B. Watson
6. Cultural relativism	Arnold Gesell
7. Natural Selection	Sigmund Freud
8. Nativism	Erik Erikson

APPLICATION

Which theory or approach can be seen as the source of each of the following bits of advice given to new parents?

1.   "Children learn the most from what you show them."

2.   "Children must be taught to distinguish right from wrong. Parents must react very differently when their children behave properly and improperly."

3.   "It doesn't matter how much you tell them. The important thing is how much they take in, remember and use."

4.   "In being a parent, it is important to do what comes naturally."

5.   "Children cannot understand ideas which are too far over their heads."

6.   "Children influence parents at least as much as parents influence children."

7.   "Children don't learn very much all by themselves."

SAMPLE TEST QUESTIONS

1. The notion of *tabula rasa* can be found in whose view of development?

    a. John Locke
    c. Jean-Jacques Rousseau
    b. Johann Gottried von Herder
    d. Charles Darwin

2. Rousseau viewed children as:

    a. born with a drive for identity
    b. a blank slate at birth
    c. born with a certain amount of sexual energy
    d. born with an innate sense of justice and fairness

3. The belief that the subject of psychology should be the study of observable behavior was held by:

    a. Gesell
    c. Piaget
    b. Watson
    d. Hall

4. Watson emphasized _____ in studying development.

    a. psychosexual stages of development
    b. how children's thinking changes across age
    c. objective, observable subject matter
    d. the development of the typical child

5. Arnold Gesell's work was primarily focused on:

    a. stages of cognitive development in children
    b. stages of psychosexual development
    c. understanding human development in terms of conditioning
    d. the development of the typical child

6. Freud's theory of development would be best described as:

    a. continuous
    c. nativistic
    b. discontinuous
    d. environmental

7. Which of Erikson's stages of development corresponds to Freud's anal stage?

    a. initiative versus guilt
    b. autonomy versus shame and doubt
    c. trust versus mistrust
    d. industry versus inferiority

8.   Most current developmental psychologists can be described as _____, in terms of their views on the nature-nurture issue.

a.	idiographologists	b.	environmentalists
c.	interactionists	d.	nativists

9.   Investigations of individual differences in children's development are characteristic of:

a.	idiographic research	b.	normative research
c.	continuity research	d.	discontinuity research

10.   In Piaget's theory, schemes are:

a.   functions that shape children's behavior
b.   sequences of stimulus-response associations
c.   cognitive structures that reflect underlying knowledge
d.   strings of commands similar to a computer program

11.   Accommodation is the tendency to:

a.   use existing knowledge in order to understand new information
b.   modify existing schemes when confronted with new information
c.   reconcile biological and environmental influences
d.   change one's behavior after a negative reinforcer

12.   The period of formal operations, unlike previous stages, features:

a.   use of symbols such as words, numbers, etc.
b.   interest in other individuals
c.   the ability to perform mental operations on bits of knowledge
d.   higher-level abstract reasoning

13.   Which would be the least interesting to a researcher working from an information-processing perspective?

a.   encoding
b.   reinforcement
c.   retrieval
d.   storage in long-term memory

14.   Research on children's learning through shared problem-solving experiences with another, such as a teacher or parent, is likely inspired by which theoretical perspective?

a.	sociocultural	b.	social learning
c.	information processing	d.	sociobiology

15. Which of the following processes is not a feature of Vygotsky's theory of development?

    a. classical conditioning of response
    b. increasing internalization of cultural knowledge
    c. language as a tool of thought
    d. shared problem solving

16. Which of the following is not a condition necessary to meet a psychologist's definition of learning?

    a. behavior must change
    b. learning must result from practice or experience
    c. learning is relatively permanent
    d. material learned must be committed to long-term memory

17. When a student has done an exceptional job on an assignment, Ms. Bigley gives him or her extra internet time on the computer as a reward and then announces this reward to the whole class, to motivate them. This is an example of:

    a. a conditioned response
    b. reciprocal determinism
    c. dialectical process
    d. vicarious reinforcement

18. Mr. Jones wants to teach his class to stay out of fights. He shows them a demonstration videotape in which the main actor refuses to be drawn into a fight even after other children ridicule him. Which process might well occur after the children see the video?

    a. observational learning
    b. reciprocal determinism
    c. dishabituation
    d. dialectical process

19. Imprinting was first extensively studied by:

    a. Bowlby   b. Bandura
    c. Lorenz   d. Bronfenbrenner

20. Bowlby's theory mixes ethology with:

    a. social learning theory
    b. information-processing theory
    c. Freudian theory
    d. Piagetian theory

Answers

Fill-in Exercises

1. tabula rasa   2. nativism   3. recapitulation   4. zeitgeist   5. norms   6. libido; erogenous zones
7. nature; nurture   8. continuity; discontinuity   9. normative; idiographic   10. genetic epistemology
11. clinical method   12. does   13. scheme   14. accommodation   15. assimilation   16. preoperational
17. concrete   18. three; computer   19. dialectical   20. internalization   21. microsystem; exosystem
22. permanent; behavior   23. operant; respondent   24. stimulus generalization   25. positive reinforcement;
punishment   26. reinforced   27. person; environment; behavior   28. mother, child (or infant); sensitive

Using What You Have Learned

1. Locke   2. Watson   3. Freud   4. Gesell   5. Erikson   6. Von Herder   7. Darwin   8. Rousseau

Application

1. social-learning theory   2. operant conditioning   3. information processing   4. human ethology
5. cognitive-developmental theory   6. ecological systems theory   7. sociocultural approach (Vygotsky)

Sample Test Questions

1. a	11. b
2. d	12. d
3. b	13. b
4. c	14. a
5. d	15. a
6. b	16. d
7. b	17. d
8. c	18. a
9. a	19. c
10. c	20. c

Chapter 2
Research Methods

OUTLINE

Use this outline as you read the chapter. Enter your questions, comments, and notes in the space provided. Write down terms or statements you don't understand, with their page numbers.

SCIENTIFIC RESEARCH

The Role of Theory

Objectivity and Measurement

TYPES OF RESEARCH

Descriptive Research

Correlational Research

Experimental Research

STUDYING DEVELOPMENT

Longitudinal Research

Classics of Research
Terman's Studies of Genius

Cross-Sectional Research

Combining Longitudinal and Cross-Sectional Research

Microgenetic Studies

On the Cutting Edge
Meta-Analysis

OTHER RESEARCH TACTICS

Case Studies

Cultural Research

Comparative Research

ETHICAL ISSUES

Potential Risks

Safeguards

LEARNING OBJECTIVES

Upon completion of Chapter 2, you should be able to discuss the following topics. Check off those you are confident that you can discuss well. Re-read the material in the text for the topics about which you are less confident. Record the important points from your reading in the space below each topic.

1.   Describe the two important roles of theory in research.

2.   Explain why objective methods are valuable in research, and discuss three ways by which investigators ensure objectivity in their research.

3.   Discuss the general strengths and limitations of each of the following measurement options in psychological research:

Observation in the natural setting

Measurement in a structured laboratory environment

Verbal report of behavior from some knowledgeable informant

4.   Explain how descriptive research, correlational research, and experimental research differ from one another.

5.   Define and give examples of the following: variable, positive correlation, negative correlation, scatter diagram.

6.   Describe how the independent and dependent variable differ from one another.

7.   Define and explain the use of reversal-replication studies.

8.   Explain the difference between longitudinal and cross-sectional research, and discuss the merits and drawbacks of each approach.

9.   Explain what is meant by a cross-sequential design, and discuss why such a design might be used.

10.   Discuss the advantages and disadvantages of the microgenetic method.

11.   What is *meta-analysis* and how is this procedure used?

12.   Discuss the major limitation of the case study approach.

13.   Describe two major approaches to studying the role of culture in behavior or development.

14.   Discuss two reasons for comparative research.

15.   Outline the 14 ethical standards for research with children, subscribed to by members of the Society for Research in Child Development.

KEY TERMS

Upon completion of Chapter 3, you should be able to define the following terms.

Scientific method   _____

_____

Theory _____

_____

Law (principle) _____

_____

Hypothesis   _____

_____

Objectivity   _____

_____

Descriptive research   _____

_____

Variable   _____

_____

Correlation _____

_____

Positive correlation _____

_____

Negative correlation _____

_____

Correlation coefficient (*r*) _____

_____

Scatter diagram _____

_____

Independent variable _____

_____

Dependent variable _____

_____

Reversal-replication (ABAB) design _____

_____

Longitudinal design _____

_____

Cross-sectional design _____

_____

Cohort effect _____

_____

Cross-sequential design _____

_____

Microgenetic method _____

_____

Meta-analysis _____

_____

Case study _____

_____

Cross-cultural studies _____

_____

Cultural psychology _____

_____

Ethnographic methods _____

_____

Comparative research _____

_____

FILL-IN EXERCISES

Fill in the word or words that best fit in the spaces below.

1.   A set of statements that describes the relationship between behavior and the factors that influence it is a _____ .

2.   A specific statement that is well supported by research evidence is called a _____ or _____ .

3.   A statement that simply postulates a relationship is called a _____ .

4.   Theories have two important roles in research. The first is to _____ research findings, while the second is to _____ new research.

5.   Three ways in which child psychology stresses objectivity in research are its focus on _____ behavior, which must be _____ , and which must also be _____ .

6.   Simply observing children and recording what is seen is called _____ research.

7.   When two variables change in the same direction, as do weight and height, the relation is described as a _____ correlation.

8.   The correlation coefficient is a number ranging between _____ and _____ that indicates the direction and _____ of a correlation between two variables.

9.   Correlations can be graphically depicted using a _____ _____ .

10.   A researcher systematically changes or manipulates one variable and looks at the effects of the manipulation on a second variable. The variable manipulated is called the _____ variable, while the variable observed is called the _____ variable.

11.   A reversal-replication design is also known as the _____ design.

12.   To study the persistence or stability of behaviors, or the effects of early experiences on later behavior, researchers employ the _____ design.

13.   A problem known as the cohort effect is sometimes found in _____ research.

14.   A research method that allows researchers to study changes in important developmental processes *as they are occurring* is the _____ method.

15.   _____ is a method of reviewing the research literature on a given topic that uses statistical procedures to establish the existence and size of effects.

16.   Cultural psychologists use _____ methods to gather as much information as possible about cultural practices and values.

17.   _____ research is conducted with nonhuman species to provide information relevant to human development.

USING WHAT YOU HAVE LEARNED

In Chapter 3, you learned about different types of research methods that are used in developmental psychology. Below you will find the names of various research methods. Identify which of these methods best describes each of the examples of research studies that follow.

Research Methods

Reversal-replication Design
Cross-sequential Design
Cross-sectional Research
Correlational Research
Longitudinal Research
Experimental Research

1.   The relation between children's grades at school and the number of hours they typically spend doing homework is examined.

2.   To determine whether taking vitamin C reduces the number of colds children get, a group of children are randomly divided into two groups: One group takes vitamin C daily, the other group takes an inert sugar pill. The number of colds they suffer over a 6-month period is measured.

3.   An author of children's books is worried that the words she uses in her story will not be understood by children of all ages. She reads the story to three groups of children -- one group is 4 years old, one is 5 years old, and one is 6 years old -- and compares between groups in terms of how many words the children don't understand.

4.   A researcher follows children's development to examine whether participating in an infant swimming class affects their attitudes towards sports when they reach elementary-school age.

5.   A parent couple wonders whether eliminating their child's before-bed drink of juice will reduce his bed-wetting. Before beginning, they record how often he wets his bed for one week. Then, they eliminate his bed-time drink for one week. They then re-introduce his bed-time drink for one week. Finally, they eliminate it again for a week. All the while, they keep a record of the number of nights he wets his bed.

6.   A researcher wants to determine the long-term effects of early instruction in reading on children's later reading and writing ability. He also wonders at what age such an early reading program might be most effective. He selects three groups of children, aged 3, 4, and 5 years old, and gives training in reading to each group. He then assesses each group's reading and writing ability two years later, and again four years later.

APPLICATION

Situation

A researcher is concerned that imitation plays a major role in children's beginning to smoke. She is particularly concerned with the role played by television characters who smoke and who are admired by children. She wants to examine whether children are likely to imitate such television models.

Questions to Answer

1.   If she wants to determine whether exposure to television models actually influences children (i.e., a cause - effect relationship), what type of research procedure should she use?

2.   How could she set up such a study?

3.   Suppose she wanted to know if imitation is more likely to occur in older children than in younger children (say, in 12-year-olds compared to 8-year-olds). What type of research procedure would she use?

4.   With reference to the 14 ethical standards listed in Table 2-2, what steps should this researcher take to ensure that her research follows ethical standards for research with children? Do you see any ethical problems with this research?

SAMPLE TEST QUESTIONS

1.   A statement that simply postulates a relationship is a:

a.	theory	b.	law
c.	principle	d.	hypothesis

2.   Descriptive research:

   a.   is used only when other research designs would be unethical
   b.   involves comparing groups of children of different ages
   c.   involves the combination of both cross-cultural and comparative research
   d.   involves no formal attempt to identify the relationships between variables

3.   The number that indicates the direction and strength of the relation between two variables is referred to as a:

a.	correlation coefficient	b.	negative correlation
c.	positive correlation	d.	scatter plot

4. A researcher is interested in the impact of television violence on aggressiveness in children. She records the number of violent shows watched over a 1-week period by a group of fourth-grade children and relates it to observations of the children's aggressiveness in the school playground. This study is **BEST** described as:

    a. cross-cultural
    b. experimental
    c. correlational
    d. comparative

5. A hypothetical study of the effects of television violence on children's aggressiveness reveals a correlation of +.83 between the number of violent shows watched each week and children's level of aggressiveness. Based on these findings, which of the following conclusions *might* be true?

    a. viewing violent television leads to aggressive behavior
    b. parents who do not allow their children to watch violent shows may discourage aggressive behavior in their children
    c. children who are more aggressive may have more of a "taste" for violent shows than those who are less aggressive
    d. all of the above

6. A major difference between an experiment and a correlational study is that in an experimental study we can determine that a _____ relation exists between two variables, whereas in a correlational study we cannot.

    a. positive
    b. causal
    c. strong
    d. direct

7. Assume an investigator has found a negative correlation between the amount of vitamin C people take and the number of colds they get. The investigator could safely conclude from this finding that:

    a. the amount of vitamin C taken and number of colds suffered are related to each other
    b. people who are immune to colds are somehow compelled to take vitamin C
    c. taking vitamin C causes people to be more immune to colds
    d. none of the above

8. A researcher is interested in the effects of watching Mr. Rogers' Neighborhood on prosocial behavior in children. She randomly assigns children to one of three groups; one group is required to watch 2 hours of Mr. Rogers' Neighborhood per week, the second group watches 4 hours, and the third group watches 6 hours. After one month, she observes the children in the playground, carefully recording all instances of prosocial behavior (e.g., sharing, helping, caring, etc.), and compares the three groups of children. This study is best described as:

    a. descriptive
    b. correlational
    c. experimental
    d. cross-cultural

9.   What is the *independent* variable in the study described in question 8?

   a.   Mr. Rogers
   b.   the amount of Mr. Rogers' Neighborhood viewed
   c.   the amount of prosocial behavior displayed by the children
   d.   the children

10.   What is the *dependent* variable in the study described in question 8?

   a.   Mr. Rogers
   b.   the amount of Mr. Rogers' Neighborhood viewed
   c.   the amount of prosocial behavior displayed by the children
   d.   the children

11.   Conducting a(n) _____ study is the only way to infer cause-effect relationships between variables.

   a.   cross-cultural   b.   comparative
   c.   cross-sequential   d.   experimental

12.   A researcher believes that sexism in men increases as they get older. He administers a scale of sexist attitudes (i.e., the higher the score, the more sexist is the individual) to a group of 20-year-old men and a group of 50-year-old men, and finds that the older group scores significantly higher than the younger group. He concludes that sexism does indeed seem to increase as men get older. What is likely a problem with the investigator's interpretation of his findings?

   a.   he has not considered the role of the cohort effect in his study
   b.   subject attrition could have played a major role in these results
   c.   the older men could have become "test wise" to the scale given to them
   d.   all of the above are likely problems in this study

13.   What type of design is the study described in question 12?

   a.   cross-sequential
   b.   cross-sectional
   c.   microgenetic
   d.   comparative

14.   An investigator wishes to determine the effect of a preschool language program on children's reading ability in elementary school. She also wants to determine what age would be best to begin the program (e.g. 3-years or 4-years old). What would be the best design to answer these questions?

   a.   longitudinal design   b.   cross-sectional design
   c.   cross-sequential design   d.   ABAB design

15.   The most appropriate design to use to determine whether children who have very few friends will develop psychological problems later in adulthood would be a:

    a.   comparative design
    b.   cross-sectional design
    c.   cross-sequential design
    d.   longitudinal design

16.   To determine infant auditory preferences, DeCasper and Fifer presented infants with a recording of their mother's voice and of a stranger's voice. They measured differences in the sucking rhythms of the infants (using a special pacifier) when presented with each of the two recordings. What is the *independent* variable in this study?

    a.   the auditory preferences of the infants
    b.   whether the recording was of mother's or a stranger's voice
    c.   the sucking rhythm of the infants
    d.   the special pacifier

17.   Which of the following is **NOT** a disadvantage of the longitudinal approach?

    a.   time consuming
    b.   the findings may be outdated by the time the study is completed
    c.   subject attrition
    d.   cohort effects

18.   Cross-cultural research:

    a.   allows researchers to investigate the universality of various phenomena in human development
    b.   identifies similarities in behaviors between human and non-human species
    c.   is frequently influenced by the cohort effect
    d.   involves a combination of longitudinal and cross-sectional designs

19.   An investigator wishes to examine the consequences of maternal prenatal use of cocaine on the developing fetus. He considers designing an experiment in which women who are pregnant would be randomly assigned to either of two conditions: in one condition they would be administered cocaine, in the other condition they would not. After examining the ethical standards of the Society for Research in Child Development, he decides not to conduct the experiment. Which ethical principle likely most strongly influenced his decision?

    a.   confidentiality
    b.   anonymity
    c.   reporting results
    d.   non-harmful procedures

20.   Studies that examine mother-infant relations in non-human species are examples of:

    a.   comparative research
    b.   cross-cultural research
    c.   life-course research
    d.   cross-sequential research

ANSWERS

FILL-IN EXERCISES

1. theory   2. law; principle   3. hypothesis   4. organize; guide   5. observable; measurable; quantifiable
6. descriptive   7. positive   8. +1.00, -1.00; strength   9. scatter diagram   10. independent; dependent
11. ABAB   12. longitudinal   13. cross-sectional   14. microgenetic   15. meta-analysis   16. ethnographic
17. comparative

USING WHAT YOU HAVE LEARNED

1. correlational research   2. experimental research   3. cross-sectional research
4. longitudinal research   5. reversal-replication design   6. cross-sequential design

APPLICATION

1. Experimental research
2. Experiment research would involve actually exposing groups of children to models who do or do not smoke (independent variable) and measuring how many children in each group imitate this behavior (dependent variable). There are serious ethical concerns with such a design. The study could also be correlational, looking for a relation between smoking in participants and in the shows they typically watch.
3. Cross-sectional design
4. The researcher needs to follow all 14 ethical standards relevant to this research. Although there are a number of serious ethical problems with this study (particularly if the experimental method is employed), Principle 1 is particularly relevant, as smoking has harmful consequences for the child. No researcher should conduct research that would encourage or result in harmful consequences to children.

SAMPLE TEST QUESTIONS

1. d	11. d
2. d	12. a
3. a	13. b
4. c	14. c
5. d	15. d
6. b	16. b
7. a	17. d
8. c	18. a
9. b	19. d
10. c	20. a

Chapter 3
Genetics: The Biological Context of Development

OUTLINE

Use this outline as you read the chapter. Enter your questions, comments, and notes in the space provided. Write down terms or statements you don't understand, with their page numbers.

MECHANISMS OF INHERITANCE

Cell Division

Inside the Chromosome

Mendel's Studies

GENETIC DISORDERS

Hereditary Disorders

Structural Defects in the Chromosome

On the Cutting Edge
The Human Genome Project

STUDYING GENE EFFECTS ON BEHAVIOR

Family Studies

Adoption Studies

Twin Studies

Combined Twin-Study and Adoption-Study Approaches

MODELS OF GENE-ENVIRONMENT INTERACTION

Gottesman's Limit-Setting Model

Scarr's Niche-Picking Model

Plomin's Environmental Genetics Model

Bronfenbrenner and Ceci's Bioecological Model

LEARNING OBJECTIVES

Upon completion of Chapter 3, you should be able to discuss the following topics. Check off those you are confident that you can discuss well. Re-read the material in the text for the topics about which you are less confident. Record the important points from your reading in the space below each topic.

1. Describe and differentiate between mitosis and meiosis.

2. Describe the importance of each of the following:

    genes

    chromosomes

    DNA

3. Explain the following principles from Mendel's theory:

    principle of dominance

    principle of segregation

    principle of independent assortment

4. Outline four revisions of Mendel's principles that have been described.

5. Describe briefly the following hereditary disorders:

    Huntington's disease

    Tay-Sachs Disease

Phenylketonuria

Sickle-Cell Anemia

6.   Outline the commonly found characteristics of Down syndrome.

7.   Describe four disorders of the sex-chromosomes:

8.   Describe how each of the following types of studies have been used to study the influence of genes on observable human traits:

family studies

adoption studies

twin studies

combined twin and adoption studies

9.   Explain how monozygotic twins differ from dizygotic twins.

10.   Explain how heredity and environment interact in Gottesman's limit-setting model.

11.   Explain the following types of gene-environment correlations described by Sandra Scarr:

passive gene-environment correlation

evocative gene-environment correlation

active gene-environment correlation

12.   Discuss how the notion of *nonshared environment* in Plomin's environmental genetics model accounts for differences in the characteristics and behavior of siblings.

13.   Explain why Bronfenbrenner and Ceci refer to their model as *bioecological*.

KEY TERMS

Upon completion of Chapter 3, you should be able to define the following terms.

Chromosomes _____

_____

Autosomes _____

_____

Sex chromosomes _____

_____

Mitosis _____

_____

Meiosis _____

_____

Crossing over _____

_____

Gene _____

_____

Deoxyribonucleic acid (DNA) _____

_____

Alleles _____

_____

Phenotype _____

_____

Genotype _____

_____

Dominant gene _____

_____

Recessive gene _____

_____

Polygenic inheritance _____

_____

Incomplete dominance _____

_____

Codominance _____

_____

Genetic imprinting _____

_____

Identical (monozygotic) twins _____

_____

Fraternal (dizygotic) twins _____

_____

Developmental pacing _____

_____

Behavior genetics _____

_____

Reaction range _____

_____

Passive gene-environment correlation _____

_____

Evocative gene-environment correlation _____

_____

Active gene-environment correlation _____

_____

Nonshared environment _____

_____

Proximal processes _____

_____

FILL-IN EXERCISES

Fill in the word or words that best fit in the spaces below.

1.   Genetic material is organized into chemical strands called _____.

2.   Body cells reproduce by the process called _____; germ cells reproduce by the process called _____.

3.   The process by which one member of a pair of chromosome exchanges genetic material with the other member is called _____ _____.

4.   The double helix describes the structure of the _____ molecule.

5.   Genes that guide the production of proteins are _____ genes. Their activities are controlled by _____ genes.

6.   The characteristic of a trait that is expressed or observable is called the _____, while the arrangement of genes underlying a trait is referred to as the _____.

7.   When neither member of a pair of genes is entirely dominant nor entirely recessive, the genes display _____ _____.

8.   _____ disease is an example of a genetic disorder caused by a dominant gene.

9.   The genetic disease where the body's ability to breakdown phenylalanine is affected is called _____.

10.   Sickle-cell anemia is caused by a _____ *(dominant/recessive)* gene.

11.   Down syndrome is the result of a structural abnormality in the _____.

12.   Identical twins are also referred to as _____ twins; fraternal twins are referred to as _____ twins.

13.   According to Gottesman's limit-setting model, genes do not determine development precisely. Instead they establish a _____ _____ within which development will occur.

14.   According to Scarr's niche-picking model, a(n) _____ gene-environment correlation refers to the situation in which genes and environment affect development similarly, because genetically-set predispositions of the child elicit comparable experiences from the environment.

15.   Plomin's model uses the term _____ environment to refer to presumed aspects of the environment that children experience differently.

16.   Bronfenbrenner and Ceci use the term _____ _____ to refer to interactions between the child and aspects of the microsystem which have positive effects on psychological functioning and which help to maximize expression of the child's genetic potential.

APPLICATION

Situation

Two students enrolled in a developmental psychology class have just read Chapter 3 in the textbook and are discussing how genes and the environment interact. One argues that heredity pretty much determines how we turn out and the environment plays a very small role. The other believes that it really is the environment that is important, particularly when considering psychological characteristics, and that heredity plays a major role only in determining physical characteristics such as body build, hair color, and so on.

Questions to Answer

1.   Can we really make statements like "heredity is more important than the environment?"

2.   What do we know about the role of heredity in psychological characteristics like intellectual performance, personality, and mental disorders?

3.   What are some of the ways that genes and the environment interact?

4.   How do psychologists go about researching the interaction between genes and the environment?

USING WHAT YOU HAVE LEARNED

In Chapter 4 you read about the role genes play in various psychological characteristics. Think of a characteristic in yourself -- maybe a particular skill or ability (e.g., mechanical ability, musical ability, mathematical ability, etc.) or a personality or temperamental characteristic. Now, take a look at your closest relatives (parents, siblings) and compare how similar they are to you in terms of the characteristic. If they are similar, could genes account for the similarity? What other influences need to be considered?

SAMPLE TEST QUESTIONS

1.   Human body cells contain how many chromosomes?

    a.   23 individual chromosomes
    b.   23 pairs of chromosomes
    c.   46 pairs of chromosomes
    d.   the number depends upon the person's gender

2.   Body cells duplicate by the process of:

    a.   dominance
    b.   crossing over
    c.   meiosis
    d.   mitosis

3.   The gametes produced as a result of meiosis contain:

    a.   23 pairs of identical chromosomes
    b.   46 individual chromosomes
    c.   either 23 pairs or 46 individual chromosomes, depending on the individual's gender
    d.   23 individual chromosomes

4.   Crossing over describes the phenomenon by which:

    a.   genetic material is exchanged between chromosomes
    b.   germ cells duplicate
    c.   body cells duplicate
    d.   certain genetic abnormalities occur

5.   The person considered the father of modern genetics is:

    a.   Gottesman
    b.   Ceci
    c.   Mendel
    d.   Huntington

6.   Phenotype refers to:

    a.   a person's inherited genetic makeup
    b.   the observable expression of one's genetic makeup
    c.   a genetic disorder that results from a problem involving the bodily management of protein
    d.   the amount of genetic material shared with members of one's immediate family

7.   Betty has blue eyes. Her parents both have brown eyes. Based on what we know about genetics, we can conclude that:

   a.   both of Betty's parents must carry a dominant gene for blue eyes
   b.   both of Betty's parents must carry a recessive gene for blue eyes
   c.   one of Betty's parents must carry a dominant gene for blue eyes
   d.   Betty cannot be the biological child of these parents

8.   What do color blindness and phenylketonuria have in common?

   a.   both are caused by a recessive gene
   b.   both are caused by a dominant gene
   c.   both are examples of incomplete dominance
   d.   neither has a genetic basis

9.   If both parents carry the gene responsible for PKU, what is the likelihood of their child having PKU?

   a.   0
   b.   1 in 10
   c.   1 in 4
   d.   3 in 4

10.   If detected early, a special diet can help with:

   a.   phenylketonuria
   b.   sickle-cell anemia
   c.   Huntington's chorea
   d.   Tay-Sachs disease

11.   Which disorder appears to be influenced by the age at which a woman becomes pregnant?

   a.   PKU
   b.   Tay-Sachs disease
   c.   Down Syndrome
   d.   Huntington's disease

12.   Monozygotic twins share what percent of the same genes?

   a.   25%
   b.   50%
   c.   75%
   d.   100%

13.   Which set of twins are no more similar in terms of genetic makeup than are any other siblings who share the same parents?

    a.   monozygotic twins
    b.   dizygotic twins
    c.   identical twins
    d.   trizygotic twins

14.   A major problem with the twin study approach is:

    a.   family environment may be more similar for monozygotic than for dizygotic twins
    b.   it is so hard to find monozygotic twins to study
    c.   it is very hard to find dizygotic twins to study
    d.   monozygotic twins are frequently the opposite sex from each other

15.   In which of the following characteristics do genetics **NOT** play a role?

    a.   intellectual performance
    b.   psychiatric disorders
    c.   personality
    d.   actually, genetics play a role in ALL of the above

16.   The pattern of spurts and plateaus in the rate of an individual's physical and mental development is referred to as:

    a.   proximal processes   b.   developmental pacing
    c.   niche-picking   d.   crossing over

17.   Which of the following findings is true of the intellectual and cognitive abilities of children living in adoptive homes?

    a.   stronger correlations have been found between the scores of adoptive children and their adoptive parents than between the children and their biological parents
    b.   stronger correlations have been found between the scores of adoptive children and their adoptive siblings than between the children and their biological siblings
    c.   stronger correlations have been found between the scores of adoptive children and their biological parents than between the children and their adoptive parents.
    d.   stronger correlations have been found between the scores of adoptive children and their adoptive fathers than between the children and their biological mothers

18.   Family studies have shown that children whose mothers have schizophrenia are about _____ times more likely to develop schizophrenia than are children of normal mothers.

    a.   5   b.   8
    c.   10   d.   30

19. The notion that genes interact with the environment by setting the upper and lower limits of our development was proposed by:

    a. Gottesman
    b. Scarr
    c. Plomin
    d. Bronfenbrenner

20. According to Sandra Scarr, during infancy genes exert their effects on the environment in a(n) _____ way.

    a. evocative
    b. active
    c. non-shared
    d. passive

ANSWERS

FILL-IN EXERCISES

1. chromosomes   2. mitosis; meiosis   3. crossing over   4. DNA   5. structural; regulator   6. phenotype; genotype   6. incomplete dominance   8. Huntington's   9. phenylketonuria (PKU)   10. recessive   11. chromosome   12. monozygotic; dizygotic   13. reaction range   14. evocative   15. nonshared   16. proximal processes

SAMPLE TEST QUESTIONS

1. b	11. c
2. d	12. d
3. d	13. b
4. a	14. a
5. c	15. d
6. b	16. b
7. b	17. c
8. a	18. c
9. c	19. a
10. a	20. d

Chapter 4
Prenatal Development

OUTLINE

Use this outline as you read the chapter. Enter your questions, comments, and notes in the space provided. Write down terms or statements you don't understand, with their page numbers.

STAGES OF PRENATAL DEVELOPMENT

Conception

The Period of the Zygote (Conception to Second Week)

The Period of the Embryo (Third to Eighth Week)

The Period of the Fetus (8th to 38th Week)

On the Cutting Edge
Families Created by Alternative Methods of Conception

TERATOLOGY

Historical Ideas

General Principles

Types of Teratogens

NATURAL CHALLENGES

Nutrition

Maternal Experiences and Stress

Parental Age

PREVENTING, DETECTING AND TREATING BIRTH DEFECTS

Prevention

Screening for Abnormalities

Treatment

Ethical Considerations

LEARNING OBJECTIVES

Upon completion of Chapter 4 you should be able to discuss the following topics. Check off those you are confident that you can discuss well. Re-read the material in the text for the topics about which you are less confident. Record the important points from your reading in the space below each topic.

1. Discuss how the zygote is created.

2. Describe what takes place during the first two weeks after conception.

3. Differentiate between the endodermal, ectodermal, and mesodermal layers of the embryo.

4. Describe how oxygen and nutrients are passed from the mother to the fetus.

5. Describe the external changes that take place during the fetal period.

6. Describe the growth of internal organs, including the nervous system and sex organs, during the fetal period.

7. Describe the early signs of behavior that have been observed in the fetus from the third through seventh months.

8.   Explain why the 23rd to 24th week of fetal age is referred to as the *age of viability*. Why are younger fetuses not able to survive if born prematurely?

9.   Discuss the physical and socioemotional implications of common alternative methods of conception.

10.   Describe the six general principles that explain how teratogens act.

11.   Describe the major abnormalities associated with prenatal use of the drug thalidomide.

12.   Describe how each of the following street drugs can affect the fetus:

Heroin

Cocaine

Marijuana

13.   Describe the major abnormalities associated with prenatal use of diethylstilbestrol (DES).

14.   Discuss the prenatal use of the following drugs:

caffeine

nicotine

alcohol

15. Discuss how environmental chemicals may have teratogenic effects, using the effects of mercury, lead, polychlorinated biphenyls (PCBs) to illustrate your points.

16. Describe the teratogenic effects of the following maternal infectious diseases:

    Rubella

    Herpes

    HIV

    Syphilis and Gonorrhea

17. Describe the effects of maternal malnutrition. Why is it difficult to isolate the effects of malnutrition from other factors?

18. Discuss how phenylketonuria in the mother can harm the fetus, even when the fetus is genetically normal.

19. Discuss the problems in interpreting the relation between prenatal stress in the mother and problems in the baby.

20. Discuss the role of parental age (both of the mother and the father) in prenatal development.

21. Discuss 4 major methods of screening for fetal abnormalities – ultrasound imaging, amniocentesis, chorionic villus sampling, and test-tube screening. What does each method involve, when can it be used during pregnancy, what problems can each reveal, and what risks, if any, does each carry?

22.   Compare 3 methods for treating birth defects -- medical therapy, surgery, and genetic engineering. How do they differ, and which holds the greatest promise?

KEY TERMS

Upon completion of Chapter 4 you should be able to define the following terms.

Conception   _____

_____

Zygote _____

_____

Embryo _____

_____

Amniotic sac   _____

_____

Placenta   _____

_____

Umbilical cord   _____

_____

Fetus   _____

_____

Age of viability _____

_____

Teratogen _____

_____

Teratology _____

_____

Fetal alcohol syndrome (FAS) _____

_____

Genetic counseling _____

_____

Ultrasound imaging _____

_____

Amniocentesis _____

_____

Chorionic villus sampling (CVS) _____

_____

FILL-IN EXERCISES

Fill in the word or words that best fit in the spaces below.

1. Prenatal development begins at _____, or fertilization, when a sperm unites with an ovum to form a single cell called a _____.

2. The period of the _____ ends about 2 weeks after fertilization. During this period, the _____ settles into the blood-enriched lining of the uterus, a process referred to as _____ .

3. The 3rd to 8th week of pregnancy is referred to as the period of the _____.

4. In the third week, the inner cell mass differentiates into three layers, from which all body structures will emerge. Internal organs and glands develop from the _____ layer. Parts of the body that maintain contact with the outside world develop from the _____ layer. Muscles, cartilage, bones, sex organs, and heart develop from the _____ layer.

5.   The _____ is the organ through which the mother and the embryo exchange materials. It is linked to the embryo via the _____ _____, which houses the blood vessels carrying these materials.

6.   The 9th to 38th week is referred to as the period of the _____.

7.   The age of _____ refers to the age at which the infant has a chance to survive if born prematurely. This age is currently around _____ to _____ weeks of fetal age.

8.   External sexual organs in males become apparent by the end of the _____ month.

9.   Fetal activity begins in the _____ month. By the _____ month, brain connections are sufficient for the fetus to exhibit a sucking reflex when the lips are touched.

10.   The discovery and study of the harmful effects of teratogens through the use of behavioral measures is referred to as _____.

11.   _____ affects the fetus indirectly through reduced maternal blood flow to the uterus, limiting the fetus's supply of nutrients and oxygen. It also passes through the placenta and into the fetus's bloodstream, affecting the fetus's heart rate, blood pressure, and chemical nerve transmitters in the brain.

12.   _____ _____ _____ refers to a unique set of features, including facial malformations and other physical and mental disabilities in the infant and child, caused by the mother's use of alcohol during pregnancy. Some children exposed prenatally to alcohol demonstrate some, but not all, of these effects. Such children are said to suffer from _____ _____ _____.

13.   Most herpes 2 infections of infants occur following direct contamination by the mother's infected _____ _____.

14   It appears that the _____ virus can be passed on to the baby directly through the placenta prior to birth and also through breast milk following birth.

15.   The fetus is relatively resistant to infection from the syphilis spirochete until the _____ or _____ month after conception.

16.   Diets lacking in _____ are associated with cretinism, a severe thyroid deficiency that causes physical stunting and mental deficiency.

17.   Achondroplasia is a genetic disorder that is related to the age of the _____.

18.   _____ _____ is a noninvasive procedure for detecting physical defects in the fetus that uses soundlike waves to provide a continuous picture of the fetus and its environment.

19.   _____ is a procedure in which a needle is passed through the mother's abdominal wall into the amniotic sac to gather discarded fetal cells to examine for chromosomal and genetic defects.

USING WHAT YOU HAVE LEARNED

Many people hold a lot of misconceptions and inaccurate beliefs about pregnancy and prenatal development. You may have encountered some of these beliefs, sometimes held by otherwise well-informed people. After reading Chapter 4 you should be able to argue against many common misconceptions about prenatal development based on what current research has shown. Listed below are some common misconceptions. Based on what you have read in Chapter 4 argue against each of these misconceptions.

1.   "The fetus is protected against any harm by the placenta and the amniotic fluid it is surrounded by."

2.   "Nutrition is not a problem for the fetus. It is sort of like a parasite: it takes whatever it needs in terms of nutrition from the mother, regardless of what she eats. Although the mother may be malnourished, the fetus is still able to meet its nutritional needs."

3.   "If a mother is frightened while pregnant, or if she has unsatisfied cravings for certain types of food, these may show up in birthmarks of a particular shape or color in the infant."

4.   "It is only 'real' drugs that a mother needs to be concerned with. People use things like alcohol, caffeine, or nicotine all the time -- they couldn't hurt the fetus."

5.   "Marijuana doesn't have any harmful effects on the mother, and it isn't addictive, so it couldn't hurt the fetus."

6.   "If a mother gets sick during pregnancy, the more severe her symptoms, the more likely the disease will affect the fetus."

7.   "With all these things around that can cause birth defects, it's better to decide not to have children. The chances of having a child with a birth defect are very high, and there's nothing you can do about it."

APPLICATION

Situation

After finishing school, you are planning to begin a family. You want your children to have the best environment to grow up in, beginning with the prenatal environment. You decide to ask your doctor's advice about pregnancy.

1.   After reading Chapter 4 what sorts of precautions do you expect your doctor to give you?

2.   If conception became a problem, what alternative methods of conception might your doctor propose?

3.   Suppose you were concerned about a genetic disorder present in some of your relatives. What might your doctor suggest to evaluate the chances that the disorder might appear in your children?

4.   Your doctor suspects twins! What screening procedures might be used to check this out?

SAMPLE TEST QUESTIONS

1.   The zygote:

   a.   receives 23 pairs of chromosomes from the mother and 23 pairs of chromosomes from the father
   b.   receives 23 chromosomes from the mother and 23 from the father
   c.   receives 23 chromosomes either from the mother or from the father, depending on the gender of the zygote
   d.   contains only 23 individual chromosomes, which will mix with 23 from another zygote at conception

2.   Implantation is a process that takes about

   a.   one week
   b.   two weeks
   c.   three weeks
   d.   four weeks

3.   The period of the embryo ends:

   a.   when implantation begins
   b.   when implantation is complete
   c.   at the end of the eighth week prenatal development
   d.   at birth

4.   Most internal organs and glands develop from:

   a.   the ectodermal layer
   b.   the mesodermal layer
   c.   the endodermal layer
   d.   the ectoplasmic layer

5.   Oxygen and nutrients pass from the mother to the fetus, and waste products pass from the fetus to the mother by way of the:

   a.   placenta
   b.   amniotic fluid
   c.   amniotic sac
   d.   birth canal

6.   The period of the fetus lasts:

   a.   from implantation until the 8th week
   b.   from implantation until birth
   c.   from the 9th week until the 24th week
   d.   from the 9th week until birth

7.   Fetal activity begins:

   a.   in the first month
   b.   in the third month
   c.   in the fifth month
   d.   in the seventh month

8.   Twenty-four weeks of age is known as:

   a.   the age of viability
   b.   the age of implantation
   c.   the end of the period of the embryo
   d.   the end of the period of the fetus

9.   The term *teratogen* describes:

   a.   a procedure for detecting possible birth defects
   b.   a method for dealing with infertility
   c.   the development of the prenatal support system -- the amniotic sac, placenta, and umbilical cord
   d.   a non-genetic agent that can cause malformation in the fetus or embryo

10.   Which of the following statements about teratogens is **NOT** true?

    a.   A teratogen's effect depends on the genetic makeup of the organism exposed to it.
    b.   The effect of a teratogen on development depends partly on timing.
    c.   Teratogens always gain access to the fetus by passing from the mother's blood to that of the fetus via the placenta.
    d.   The likelihood and degree of abnormal development increase with the dosage and degree of exposure.

11.   Teratogens are **most** likely to affect organ development:

    a.   during the period of the zygote
    b.   during the period of the embryo
    c.   during the period of the fetus
    d.   just before implantation

12.   During which of the following periods of prenatal development are the effects of Rubella most severe?

    a.   the first month post-conception
    b.   the second month post-conception
    c.   the third month post-conception
    d.   the fourth month post-conception

13.   Which of the following statements is true concerning the prenatal effects of nicotine?

    a.   The effects of nicotine and smoke on the fetus have not yet been investigated.
    b.   Smoking during pregnancy produces a unique set of malformations in the fetus know as the "fetal nicotine syndrome."
    c.   Smoking has been clearly associated with physical defects, such as limb (arm and leg) defects, particularly during the early stages of pregnancy.
    d.   Smokers, on average, have smaller babies that face an increased risk of infant mortality.

14.   The symptoms of fetal alcohol syndrome include:

    a.   a predisposition toward alcoholism
    b.   increased risk for PKU
    c.   mental retardation and learning disabilities
    d.   increased risk for Down syndrome

15.   The disease that most frequently affects the fetus as it passes through the birth canal is:

    a.   cytomegalovirus   b.   herpes 2
    c.   HIV   d.   rubella

16. The fetus is relatively resistant to _____ until the fourth or fifth month post-conception.

   a. herpes 2
   b. syphilis
   c. HIV
   d. cytomegalovirus

17. Which of the following disorders is related to the age of the father?

   a. herpes 2
   b. HIV
   c. rubella
   d. achondroplasia

18. Which of the following statements is true concerning the effects of prenatal anxiety?

   a. Research reveals that a relation exists between maternal prenatal anxiety and later problems in the offspring.
   b. Although the belief that maternal anxiety could affect the fetus is quite old, current research indicates that this is simply not true.
   c. Although anxiety may have psychological effects on the fetus, it cannot produce physical effects.
   d. Experimental evidence has virtually ruled out the role of genetic factors in the effect of maternal anxiety on the fetus.

19. The procedure in which a small tube is inserted through the cervix and into the placenta to collect a small sample of fetal cells is referred to as:

   a. amniocentesis
   b. ultrasound imaging
   c. chorionic villus sampling
   d. test tube screening

20. Which of the following is **NOT** true about ultrasound imaging?

   a. The sex of the fetus can be determined using this procedure.
   b. This procedure can determine if there is more than one fetus.
   c. Defects of the heart, bladder, and kidneys can be revealed using this approach.
   d. There is an increased risk of miscarriage associated with this approach.

ANSWERS

FILL-IN EXERCISES

1. conception; zygote   2. zygote; zygote; implantation   3. embryo   4. endodermal, ectodermal, mesodermal   5. placenta; umbilical cord   6. fetus   7. viability; 23, 24   8. third   9. third; seventh   10. psychoteratology   11. cocaine   12. fetal alcohol syndrome; fetal alcohol effects   13. birth canal   14. HIV   15. fourth, fifth   16. iodine   17. father   18. ultrasound imaging   19. amniocentesis

SAMPLE TEST QUESTIONS

1. b	11. b
2. a	12. a
3. c	13. d
4. c	14. c
5. a	15. b
6. d	16. b
7. b	17. d
8. a	18. a
9. d	19. c
10. c	20. d

Chapter 5
Physical Development:
Birth, Motor Skills, and Growth

OUTLINE

Use this outline as you read the chapter. Enter your questions, comments, and notes in the space provided. Write down terms or statements you don't understand, with their page numbers.

BIRTH AND THE PERINATAL PERIOD

Labor and Delivery

Cultural Attitudes toward Birth

The Concept of Risk

THE ORGANIZED NEWBORN

States of alertness

Applications
Sudden Infant Death Syndrome

Rhythms

Reflexes

Congenitally Organized Behaviors

MOTOR DEVELOPMENT

Principles and Sequences

The Nature and Nurture of Motor-Skills Development

Classics of Research
Does Motor Development Depend on Practice or Maturation

The Psychological Implications of Motor Development

Motor Development in Childhood

THE HUMAN BRAIN

Structure of the Brain

Development of the Brain

Hemispheric Specialization

Studying the Brain

PHYSICAL GROWTH

Growth in Size

Changes in Body Proportion and Composition

Puberty

Factors that Affect Growth and Maturation

LEARNING OBJECTIVES

Upon completion of Chapter 5, you should be able to discuss the following topics. Check off those you are confident that you can discuss well. Re-read the material in the text for the topics about which you are less confident. Record the important points from your reading in the space below each topic.

1.   Describe the three stages of labor.

2.   Contrast the Western attitude toward birth with that of other cultures.

3.   Discuss the following three indicators of risk for developmental delay and cognitive and social problems:

maternal and family characteristics

physical compromise of the newborn

physical and behavioral assessments

4.   Contrast preterm babies with SGA babies.

5.   Describe the following assessment tools: Apgar Exam and Brazelton Neonatal Behavioral Assessment.

6.   Discuss how "prematurity stereotyping" may affect parents' perceptions of their infants.

7.   Describe Wolff's states of infant alertness and explain how they can provide information about an infant's development.

8.   Explain what *sudden infant death syndrome* refers to and discuss several risk factors related to this syndrome.

9.   Explain how the newborn's rhythms may affect sleep patterns.

10.   Differentiate between *reflexes* and *congenitally organized behaviors*, providing examples of each and describing their significance in an infant's development.

11.   Describe each of the following reflexes and indicate the age at which each disappears:

rooting reflex

palmar reflex

Moro reflex

stepping reflex

12.   Discuss each of the following congenitally organized behaviors:

looking

sucking

crying

13.   Explain the principles of *proximodistal* and *cephalocaudal* development, giving examples of each.

14.   Discuss how nature and nurture contribute to motor development, according to the dynamic systems approach.

15.   How did Gesell use the co-twin control method to assess the roles of nature and nurture in motor development?

16.   What role does motor development play in infants' understanding of their world?

17.   Explain how information is passed along the neuron, discussing the importance of the dendrites, axon, myelin sheath, synapse, and neurotransmitters.

18.   Briefly indicate the importance of each of the following parts of the brain:

brain stem

midbrain

cerebrum

cerebral cortex

19.   Describe the following three stages of brain development:

cell production

cell migration

cell elaboration

20.   Explain how the left and right hemispheres of the brain are specialized for different tasks.

21.   Discuss how growth rates differ between boys and girls.

22.   Discuss how growth rate changes across age in terms of body proportion and composition.

23.   Discuss the physical changes that occur at puberty and how adolescents react to these changes.

24.   Discuss how heredity and nutrition affect growth and maturation.

25.   Describe each of the following eating disorders:

anorexia nervosa

bulimia

obesity

26.   Describe how abuse and psychological trauma can affect physical growth.

KEY TERMS

Upon completion of Chapter 5, you should be able to define the following terms.

Perinatal period _____

_____

Fetal distress   _____

_____

Caesarian section   _____

_____

At risk   _____

_____

Anoxia _____

_____

Preterm_____

_____

Small for gestational age (SGA) _____

_____

Apgar exam   _____

_____

Brazelton Neonatal Behavioral Assessment Scale   _____

_____

Electroencephalograph (EEG)   _____

_____

Rapid eye movement (REM) sleep _____

_____

Reflex _____

_____

Congenitally organized behavior _____

_____

Postural development _____

_____

Locomotion _____

_____

Prehension _____

_____

Proximodistal _____

_____

Cephalocaudal _____

_____

Dynamic systems approach _____

_____

Neuron _____

_____

Dendrite _____

_____

Axon _____

_____

Myelin _____

_____

Synapse _____

_____

Neurotransmitter _____

_____

Brain stem _____

_____

Midbrain _____

_____

Cerebrum _____

_____

Cerebral cortex _____

_____

Catch-up growth _____

_____

Skeletal maturity (bone age) _____

_____

Puberty _____

_____

Anorexia nervosa   _____

_____

Bulimia _____

_____

Obesity _____

_____

FILL-IN EXERCISES

Fill in the word or words that best fit in the spaces below.

1.   Labor typically begins around _____ weeks after conception.

2.   By the end of the _____ stage of labor, contractions are very intense and occur every 2-3 minutes.

3.   The procedure in which the baby is surgically removed from the uterus is referred to as _____ _____.

4.   Around 85% of the risk of severe development problems can be attributed to what happens in the _____ period of development.

5.   _____ birth-weight babies are about 40 times more likely to die in the first months of life than babies born at normal weight.

6.   The infant state of _____ _____ is characterized by regular breathing, with eyes closed and no eye movements, and no activity except for occasional jerky movements.

7.   The infant state of _____ _____ is characterized by eyes open and bright, attention focused on stimuli, and relatively low activity level.

8.   Absence of a baby's reflexive responses to external stimuli may indicate _____ to the central nervous system.

9.   Stroking a newborn's cheek causes it to turn its head toward the side that was stroked, a reflex known as the _____ reflex.

10.   The Moro reflex occurs in response to either a sudden _____, or a sudden loss of head support.

11.   Sucking can be viewed as a _____ _____ behavior.

12.   The high frequency of _____ activity during infant sleep may help keep nerve pathways active.

13.   An infant's ability to lift and hold her head before she can walk reflects the principle that development proceeds in a _____ direction.

14.   By _____ months, a baby should be able to grasp a marble with her thumb and forefinger.

15.   The ability to use the hands as tools for such things as eating, building, and exploring is referred to as _____.

16.   Thelen has found that as infants try to assemble a new motor behavior from the abilities currently available to them, they go through the following two steps: _____ and _____.

17.   The brain contains approximately _____ neurons which each have, on average, _____ connections with other cells.

18.   Most neurons are produced between _____ and _____ weeks following conception.

19.   _____ refers to an eating disorder that involves binging on large quantities of food and then vomiting to purge the excess calories consumed.

20.   Obesity is usually defined as weight that is _____ or more over a standard weight for height.

APPLICATION

Situation

Your friend has just given birth to a preterm infant, Peter, at 34 weeks gestation. She knows that you are studying developmental psychology and calls you with the following concerns:

1.   Ever since she was told that Peter scored below average on the Brazelton scale, your friend has been worried that Peter won't be as smart as his sisters and that he'll do poorly in school. How would you reassure her?

2.   The hospital staff is encouraging your friend to visit and hold Peter but she's afraid of hurting him as he looks so weak. Based on your knowledge from Chapter 5, what would you advise her to do?

3.   Your friend heard somewhere that preterm babies will always lag behind full-term babies developmentally. What does research show about the long-term development of such babies?

4.   Your friend continues to compare her baby to her sister's full-term baby, Susie, who was born one week after Peter. Although Peter is older, your friend notices that Susie is easier to soothe and looks stronger. She is concerned that this means Peter has "failure to thrive" syndrome. What do you think?

USING WHAT YOU HAVE LEARNED

Inaccurate beliefs about newborns and their development are common. Many beliefs are based on a person's experiences and are not supported by empirical evidence. Using your knowledge from this chapter, argue against the misconceptions listed below.

1.   "Infants are born without any abilities. Every one of their movements has to be learned from their parents."

2.   "Good parents should be able to get their newborn infant to sleep through the night without waking. If your infant wakes up, it is because you are spoiling him."

3.   "My baby doesn't love me any more. Last month, when I pressed my finger into her hand, she squeezed it tightly. Now she just ignores it."

4.   "Babies cry all of the time. Their crying doesn't mean anything."

5.   "All babies learn to walk the same way. If your baby doesn't crawl before he walks, he'll never walk properly."

SAMPLE TEST QUESTIONS

1. The method or preparing for childbirth using breathing and muscle exercises is attributable to:

   a. Dr. Virginia Apgar
   b. Dr. F. Lemaze
   c. Dr. Barry Brazelton
   d. none of the above

2. Fetal distress during the birth process is indicated by:

   a. unusually loud crying by the infant
   b. breech birth
   c. unusually high or low fetal heart rate
   d. a detached placenta

3. For the low-birth-weight infant, which function is most likely to be problematic?

   a. elimination of waste
   b. independence of blood circulation
   c. breathing
   d. eating

4. Health care professionals use the Brazelton Neonatal Behavioral Assessment Scale primarily to:

   a. predict future intelligence
   b. obtain a sense of the baby's well-being and risk
   c. determine which infants will need special monitoring during the first days of life
   d. assess the level of fetal distress

5. A factor that determines whether infants at risk can achieve normal development is:

   a. auditory and movement stimulation
   b. reduced parental stress
   c. positive parent-child relationship
   d. all of the above

6. When sleeping, a fetus of 25-weeks gestation engages almost exclusively in:

   a. active sleep
   b. REM sleep
   c. passive sleep
   d. a & b

7.   The purpose of REM sleep in early infancy is to:

   a.   regulate respiration
   b.   exercise the eye muscles
   c.   stimulate nerve pathways
   d.   stimulate growth of brain cells.

8.   As the infant gets older, time spent in active sleep:

   a.   increases
   b.   decreases
   c.   increases then decreases
   d.   does not change

9.   Which statement about the sleep-wake cycle of infants is true?

   a.   it is governed primarily by environmental influences
   b.   newborn cycles of active and quiet sleep are about the same in duration as adult cycles
   c.   by four months of age, the pattern of sleeping at night and being awake during the day is clearly established
   d.   all of the above are true

10.   The absence of the Moro reflex at birth:

   a.   indicates disturbance of the central nervous system
   b.   reflects normal neurological development
   c.   occurs with all full-term infants
   d.   indicates that the infant is ready to walk

11.   Congenitally-organized behaviors are unlike reflexes in that they:

   a.   do not occur in response to specific stimuli
   b.   occur in response to specific stimuli
   c.   disappear as the infant develops
   d.   are learned through modeling

12.   Which principle is illustrated by infants' ability to reach for a toy with all fingers extended before they are able to pick it up using their forefinger and thumb?

   a.   proximodistal development
   b.   cephalocaudal development
   c.   prehension
   d.   dynamic systems analysis

13.   One of the functions of the myelin sheath surrounding the axon is to:

       a.   protect adjacent axons from dendrites
       b.   speed axonal message transmission
       c.   provide a reservoir for neurotransmitters
       d.   receive activity from nearby cells and conduct it to the neurons

14.   The part of the brain responsible for balance and coordination is the:

       a.   brain stem
       b.   midbrain
       c.   cerebrum
       d.   cerebral cortex

15.   _____ continues years after the birth of the infant.

       a.   Cell production
       b.   Cell migration
       c.   Cell elaboration
       d.   none of the above

16.   Which statement about the development of the primary motor area is false?

       a.   It is the first area of the cerebral cortex to mature.
       b.   Maturation of this area can be indexed by myelin formation.
       c.   Locations that control the head and arms mature before locations controlling the legs and
             fingers.
       d.   Development follows in a proximodistal progression, but not in a cephalocaudal manner.

17.   Which of the following statements is false?

       a.   The left side of the brain is more active during language tasks and the right side more
             active during mathematical tasks.
       b.   Tasks such as reading and listening involve both sides of the brain.
       c.   Problems with reading performance are sometimes associated with right-side dominance
             for language.
       d.   Hemispheric specialization appears late in childhood, just before puberty.

18.   The effect of genetic factors on growth is illustrated by the fact that:

       a.   MZ twins show more similar pace of bone development than do DZ twins
       b.   Asian, European, and African children reach puberty at different ages and move through
             puberty at different rates
       c.   children with recessive genes achieve smaller stature than children with dominant genes
       d.   a & b

19.   In addition to contributing to slower growth, undernutrition may interfere with:

    a.   intellectual development
    b.   social stimulation
    c.   production of brain cells, brain protein, and myelin
    d.   all of the above

20.   Anorexia nervosa is:

    a.   an eating disorder involving food binging and purging
    b.   an eating disorder involving excessive weight loss through starvation
    c.   an eating disorder defined as weight 20% or more <u>below</u> a standard weight for height
    d.   none of the above

ANSWERS

FILL-IN EXERCISES

1. 38   2. first   3. Caesarian section   4. prenatal   5. Low   6. deep sleep   7. alert inactivity   8. damage
9. rooting   10. sound   11. congenitally organized   12. REM   13. cephalocaudal   14. nine   15. prehension
16. exploration; selection   17. 100 billion; 3,000   18. 10; 26   19. bulimia   20. 20%

APPLICATION

1. Although the Brazelton Scale does a fairly good job of characterizing how a baby is doing in the early period, it is not a good predictor, of later development.
2. Various forms of gentle stimulation, including rocking and gentle massage, appear to assist the early development of low-birth-weight babies. Handling the infant also increases the mother's confidence in her ability to care for the infant
3. Development in the preterm baby may lag behind that in a full-term baby, at least for a time. The resources available to the family can also be important. By 2 to 3 years of age, children born preterm into families that have strong financial resources seem indistinguishable from children born at term
4. It is important to avoid *prematurity stereotyping,* the tendency to expect negative behavior from premature infants, which can affect how parents interact with the infant.

USING WHAT YOU HAVE LEARNED

1. Newborns possess a number of reflexes and congenitally organized behaviors.
2. Newborns states occur as internally controlled rhythms that gradually adapt to the 24-hour light-dark cycle.
3. The grasping response is a reflex – it increases during the 1st moth and then gradually declines and is gone by 3 to 4 months.
4. There seem to be 3 types of crying in the very young infant: a hungry or basic cry, a mad or angry cry, and a pain cry.
5. Some babies never crawl before walking.

SAMPLE TEST QUESTIONS

1. b	11. a
2. c	12. a
3. c	13. b
4. b	14. a
5. d	15. c
6. a	16. d
7. c	17. d
8. b	18. d
9. c	19. d
10. a	20. b

Chapter 6
Sensory and Perceptual Development

OUTLINE

Use this outline as you read the chapter. Enter your questions, comments, and notes in the space provided. Write down terms or statements you don't understand, with their page numbers.

ISSUES IN THE STUDY OF PERCEPTUAL DEVELOPMENT

TOUCH AND PAIN, SMELL AND TASTE, MOTION AND BALANCE

Touch and Pain

Smell and Taste

Vestibular Sensitivity

HEARING

Prenatal Hearing

Sensitivity to Sound

Discriminating Sounds

Sound Localization

VISION

Sensory Capabilities

Classics of Research
What do Babies See? The Work of Robert Fantz

Visual Pattern and Contrast

Visual Relations

Face Perception

On the Cutting Edge
Can Newborns Recognize the Mothers' Faces?

Objects and Their Properties

The Spatial Layout

INTERMODAL PERCEPTION

Exploratory Intermodal Relations

Intermodal Representation

ATTENTION AND ACTION

Infancy

Older Children

Applications
ADHD: Helping Children with Attentional Problems

LEARNING OBJECTIVES

Upon completion of Chapter 6, you should be able to discuss the following topics. Check off those you are confident that you can discuss well. Re-read the material in the text for the topics about which you are less confident. Record the important points from your reading in the space below each topic.

1.   Distinguish between the processes of sensation, perception, and attention.

2.   Discuss how perceptual development can be viewed as involving both nature and nurture.

3.   Discuss how touch is important for relations between children and adults.

4.   Discuss the likes and dislikes of newborns in terms of smell and taste.

5.   Discuss how investigators have examined the relation between vestibular and visual perception in infants.

6.   Explain how researchers have used the habituation-dishabituation procedure to assess infant abilities to differentiate sounds.

7.   Discuss how researchers have concluded that the fetus can hear.

8.   Discuss the hearing abilities of infants, in terms of sensitivity to sound, ability to distinguish differences in intensity and frequency, and ability to localize sound.

9.   Discuss how researchers have assessed visual acuity in newborns and what we know about the visual acuity of infants.

10.   Explain how Robert Fantz examined visual preferences in infants.

11.   Discuss the peripheral vision, and color vision of infants.

12.   Describe how researchers have examined whether newborns are attracted to human faces. Can newborns recognize their mother's face?

13.   What are the visual constancies? Discuss how researchers have assessed *size constancy* in infants.

14.   Describe what researchers have found concerning *object continuity* in infant perception.

15.   Explain how the visual cliff has been used to assess infant depth perception.

16.   Describe and explain the differences between 2-month-old and 9-month-old infants in their reaction to the visual cliff.

17.   Indicate how crawling may be related to fear of height.

18.   Explain how infants use pictorial cues and kinetic cues to perceive depth.

19.   Describe what Linda Acredolo found concerning how 6-, 11-, and 16-month-old babies use landmarks for keeping track of locations in space.

20.   Explain what is meant by the term *prepared relations*?

21.   Discuss the ability of infants to form haptic-visual and auditory-visual intermodal representations.

22.   Discuss the importance of the following in controlling the infant's attention:

attention getting versus *attention holding*

absolute versus *relative* properties of stimulation

23.   List the 5 rules for acting govern the looking activity of newborns.

24.   Describe four important aspects of attention that, according to Flavell (1985), develop with age.

25.   Outline the contributions of both nature and nurture to ADHD.

26.   Describe how action skills develop through the school years.

KEY TERMS

Upon completion of Chapter 6, you should be able to define the following terms.

Sensation _____

_____

Perception _____

_____

Attention _____

_____

Haptic perception _____

_____

Vestibular sensitivity _____

_____

Visual acuity _____

_____

Visual accommodation _____

_____

Peripheral vision _____

_____

Size constancy _____

_____

Shape constancy _____

_____

Brightness constancy _____

_____

Color constancy _____

_____

Visual cliff _____

_____

Pictorial cues _____

_____

Kinetic cues _____

_____

Motion parallax _____

_____

Orienting reflex _____

_____

Defensive reflex _____

_____

Selective attention _____

_____

Attention-deficit hyperactivity disorder (ADHD) _____

_____

FILL-IN EXERCISES

Fill in the word or words that best fit in the spaces below.

1. The detection and discrimination of sensory information is referred to as _____, whereas the interpretation of sensations is referred to as _____.

2. The soothing properties of rocking and jiggling clearly demonstrate _____ sensitivity in the newborn.

3. Electrical recordings of brain responses demonstrate sound reception in fetuses as early as the _____ week after conception.

4. Newborns hear relatively better at _____ (*low/high*) frequencies.

5. As the size of an infant's head increases with age, the distance between the two ears also increases. This requires an appropriate _____ on the part of the infant in order to localize sounds accurately.

6. The visual acuity of normal adults is around 20/20. The newborn's visual acuity has been estimated at about _____ to _____. By _____ months of age, the visual acuity of infants approximates that of adults.

7. In terms of color vision, newborns can discriminate both _____ and _____ from white.

8. Looking at a face, young infants tend to look near the _____ of the face, paying relatively little attention to the _____ detail.

9. As an object moves father away from us, its image in the eye shrinks. Yet, the object continues to appear the same size. This phenomenon is called _____ _____.

10. Gibson and Walk assessed infants' perceptions of depth using the _____ _____, a unique device with an apparent drop off.

11. In perceiving depth, infants can make some use of kinetic depth cues between _____ and _____ months of age. Response to pictorial static cues is not evident until _____ to _____ months.

12. Inborn relations between sensory modes -- that is, relations for which the baby is predisposed by biology, but that are modifiable by experience -- are referred to as _____ relations.

13. After sucking on either a nubby or smooth nipple, 1-month-old infants stared longer at a picture of the nipple they had sucked. This demonstrates intermodal transfer between _____ and _____ perception.

14.   _____ attention refers to concentration on a stimulus or event with attendant disregard for other stimuli or events.

15.   In terms of controlling the infant's attention, it is useful to distinguish between aspects of stimulation are effective at attention getting, and those that are effective at attention _____.

16.   Flavell identified four important aspects of attention that develop with age: _____, _____, _____, and _____.

17.   Approximately _____% of children with ADHD have a relative with ADHD, usually a parent or sibling, suggesting that ADHD may have a biological component.

USING WHAT YOU HAVE LEARNED

1.   William James, the "father" of psychology in America, described the newborn's reaction to the world as "one great blooming, buzzing confusion." * Based on what you have read about infant sensory and perceptual abilities, how would you reply to James's description?

2.   The text warns against attributing too much skill to the infant (i.e., the "superbaby" craze). Are there abilities that do seem fairly well-developed at birth? What abilities do you think people might be inclined to overestimate in the young infant?

3.   Not long ago, hospitals routinely operated on newborns without anesthetic, under the assumption that newborns cannot feel pain. Based on what you have read in chapter 6 about the newborn's sensory abilities, what is your opinion about such practices.

APPLICATION

Situation

It is common in many cultures for mothers to sing lullabies to their babies. While there seems to be little doubt that mothers enjoy singing to their babies, babies cannot tell us whether they likewise enjoy the lullabies -- or can they?

1.   Based on your knowledge of infant auditory perception, is there any evidence that would lead us to believe that babies would enjoy hearing their mother sing to them?

2.   Following examples of research from the text, such as the work of DeCasper and Fifer, how would you design a study to examine whether infants enjoy hearing lullabies sung by their mother?

3.   Suppose you find that babies do enjoy it when their mothers sing to them. How could you test whether it is the music that they like or the fact that is their mother's voice singing?

---

* *James, W. (1890). The principles of psychology. New York: Henry Holt, p 488.*

4.   In terms of research in auditory-visual relations and facial perception, what sorts of behaviors on the part of the baby might serve to reinforce the mother's singing to the baby (assuming, of course, that the baby is awake)?

SAMPLE TEST QUESTIONS

1.   The detection and discrimination of sensory information is known as:

    a.   sensation   b.   perception
    c.   attention   d.   identification

2.   Which of the following examples best describes perception?

    a.   the ability to distinguish a high tone from a low tone
    b.   the recognition of a particular song
    c.   not noticing the words of a song because the individual is attending to its tune
    d.   identifying the musical instrument that is playing a tune

3.   Which individual(s) would be most likely to answer "Yes" to Molyneux's question whether a man born blind, who is suddenly able to see, would be able to recognize by sight what he had come to know by touch alone?

    a.   James and Eleanor Gibson   b.   John Locke
    c.   Oliver Sachs   d.   none of the above

4.   The earliest that sensitivity to touch can be seen is:

    a.   immediately at birth   b.   by the end of the first week after birth
    c.   by one month of age   d.   even before birth

5.   Infants appear able to recognize the odor of their mother:

    a.   immediately after birth
    b.   even prior to birth
    c.   within the first week of life
    d.   this ability emerges slowly across the first four months of life

6.   The soothing properties of rocking and jiggling for crying babies demonstrate:

    a.   haptic perception   b.   vestibular sensitivity
    c.   proximal stimulation   d.   recalibration

7.   Which of the following is **NOT** effective in soothing crying babies?

    a.   speaking to the infant in a high tone   b.   speaking to the infant in a low tone
    c.   placing a hand on the infant's chest   d.   gently stroking an infant

8.   Research by DeCasper and colleagues concerning newborns' auditory preferences demonstrated all of the following except:

    a.   newborns showed a preference for their mother's voice
    b.   newborns showed a preference for their father's voice
    c.   newborns showed a preference for a familiar over a novel story
    d.   actually, **all** of the above were found to be true

9.   Newborns of French-speaking mothers can discriminate French from Russian, even when spoken by the same woman. This finding indicates that:

    a.   the fetus is listening to and picking up information about the sounds its mother makes
    b.   the nativist view applies to language; infants have a preference for their "native" language
    c.   French is likely a more basic language than Russian
    d.   certain languages are much easier for newborns to understand than other languages

10.   Compared with normal adult visual acuity of 20/20, the acuity of a newborn is around 20/400 to 20/800. But, by three months of age it is:

    a.   20/20   b.   20/100
    c.   20/200   d.   20/300

11.   Which of the following is true?

    a.   newborns show a preference for the high contrast borders of a face
    b.   newborns prefer their mother's face over that of a stranger
    c.   newborns are fascinated by the internal features of a face
    d.   newborns prefer color photographs of faces over black and white photographs

12.   Recent research has found that newborns may recognize their mother's face:

    a.   by attending to the inner details of the face
    b.   by attending to her eyes alone
    c.   by attending to her hairline and the shape of her head
    d.   newborns <u>cannot</u> recognize their mother's face

13.   To date, research indicates that some _____ constancy is present at birth.

    a.   size   b.   shape
    c.   color   d.   both a and b

14.   Visual accommodation -- the automatic adjustment of the lens of the eye to produce a focused image of an object -- is almost adult-like by what age?

   a.   by the end of the first week   b.   by one month
   c.   by three months   d.   by six months

15.   Infants as young as _____ notice the difference between the deep and safe sides of the visual cliff, though they may not react with fear.

   a.   one month   b.   two months
   c.   three months   d.   four months

16.   When moved from the safe side to the deep side of the visual cliff, the heart rate of _____ increased.

   a.   2-month olds   b.   5-month olds
   c.   9-month olds   d.   12-month olds

17.   All of the following help babies to perceive depth, except

   a.   motion parallax   b.   pictorial cues
   c.   kinetic cues   d.   recalibration

18.   Flavell identified four important aspects of attention that increase with age. Which of the following is NOT one of those four aspects?

   a.   planfulness   b.   adjusting
   c.   adaptability   d.   accommodation

19.   When an experimenter asks children to judge whether two complex pictures are the same, older children systematically compare each detail across pictures, one by one. This aspect of attention is described by Flavell as:

   a.   accommodation   b.   adaptability
   c.   planfulness   d.   adjusting

20.   Which of the following is NOT true of ADHD?

   a.   children usually outgrow ADHD by adolescence
   b.   ADHD runs in families
   c.   ADHD may be associated with abnormalities in the frontal lobes of the cortex
   d.   boys are diagnosed with ADHD more often than girls

ANSWERS

FILL-IN EXERCISES

1. sensation; perception   2. vestibular   3. 25th   4. low   5. recalibration   6. 20/400; 20/800; 12 months
7. red; green   8. borders; interior   9. size constancy   10. visual cliff   11. one, three; six, seven
12. prepared   13. haptic; visual   14. selective   15. holding   16. control, adaptability, planfulness,
adjusting   17. 50

APPLICATION

1.   Newborns show a preference for their mother's voice.
2.   Present recording of lullaby and use sucking rate to measure preference.
3.   Present mother singing vs. simply the melody of the lullaby. Or, present mother versus stranger
       singing same lullaby.
4.   Infant may orient, look towards mother's face, track movements, etc.

SAMPLE TEST QUESTIONS

1. a	11. a
2. b	12. c
3. a	13. d
4. d	14. d
5. c	15. b
6. b	16. c
7. a	17. d
8. b	18. d
9. a	19. c
10. b	20. a

Chapter 7
Cognitive Development:
The Piagetian Approach

OUTLINE

Use this outline as you read the chapter. Enter your questions, comments, and notes in the space provided. Write down terms or statements you don't understand, with their page numbers.

PIAGET'S THEORY

COGNITION DURING INFANCY: THE SENSORIMOTOR PERIOD

Studying Infant Intelligence

The Six Substages

Object Permanence

Testing Piaget's Claims: More Recent Work on Infant Cognition

An Overall Evaluation

THOUGHT IN THE PRESCHOOLER: THE PREOPERATIONAL PERIOD

More about Representation

Strengths of Preoperational Thought

Limitations of Preoperational Thought

MIDDLE CHILDHOOD INTELLIGENCE: THE CONCRETE OPERATIONAL PERIOD

A Sampling of Tasks

The Concept of Operations

More on the Preoperational-Concrete Operational Contrast

ADOLESCENT AND ADULT: THE FORMAL OPERATIONAL PERIOD

Characteristics of Formal Operational Thought

A Research Example: Reasoning about Pendulums

More Recent Work on Formal Operations

GENERAL ISSUES

Stages

Universality

Cognitive Change

Applications
Piaget and Education

NEW DIRECTIONS

Concepts

Applications
Beliefs about the Causes of Illness

Theory of Mind

On the Cutting Edge
Theory of Mind in Infancy

LEARNING OBJECTIVES

Upon completion of Chapter 7 you should be able to discuss the following topics. Check off those you are confident that you can discuss well. Re-read the material in the text for the topics about which you are less confident. Record the important points from your reading in the space below each topic.

1.   Explain Piaget's use of the following ideas in his views of the structure and function of intelligence:

       Organization

       Adaptation

       Development

2.   Differentiate between *assimilation* and *accommodation.*

3.   Describe the four periods of development in Piaget's theory.

4.   Describe how Piaget combined naturalistic observation with experimental manipulation in his study of infants.

5.   Identify and describe the six substages of the sensorimotor period, providing ages for each substage.

6.   Summarize what Piaget's research revealed about the notion of object permanence.

7.   Explain the two general themes in Piaget's approach that are illustrated by his work on object permanence: *progressive decentering* and the importance of *invariants*.

8.   Explain how recent researchers have further investigated object permanence and summarize their findings.

9.   Discuss the findings of recent research examining the infant's physical knowledge and ability to imitate.

10.   Identify the five kinds of behavior that Piaget described as evidence of the capacity for representational functioning emerging near the end of infancy.

11.   Discuss the strengths and limitations of preoperational thought.

12.   Explain what Piaget means by *egocentrism* in preoperational thinking. How would this be reflected in children's responses to the three-mountains problem?

13.   Explain how *centration* affects preoperational children's responses to conservation problems.

14.   Describe a typical Piagetian conservation task and discuss the differences between the responses of a preoperational and a concrete operational child.

15.   Describe the performance of the preoperational child on problems involving class inclusion, seriation, and transitivity.

16.   Summarize the major differences between preoperational and concrete operational thought.

17.   Explain what Piaget means by the concept of *operations.*

18.   Discuss what recent research has revealed concerning preoperational children's limitations in the areas of perspective taking, symbolic activity, and conservation. Is young children's thinking as deficient as Piaget claimed?

19.   Summarize the major differences between concrete operational and formal operational thought.

20.   Describe how an adolescent capable of formal operational thought would likely go about solving the pendulum problem.

21.   Discuss what recent research has revealed concerning how the tasks used by Piaget assess formal operational reasoning.

22.   State what theorists mean by *stages* of development. Summarize the three criteria that a stage theory must meet.

23.   Discuss what cross-cultural research reveals concerning the universality of Piaget's theory of cognitive development.

24.   Summarize Piaget's views of the contributions of the following four general factors to cognitive change:

Biological Maturation

Physical Experience

Social Experience

Equilibration

25.   Explain how equilibration relates to the following aspects of development: organization, motivation, and directionality.

26.   Describe four principles that are often cited in discussions of Piagetian approaches to education.

27.   Discuss the relevance of recent research on children's *concepts* to Piaget's view of the limitations of preoperational thought.

28   Discuss what is meant by *Theory of Mind*, making reference to preoperational children's understanding of *false beliefs* and the *appearance-reality distinction*.

29.   Explain the relevance of children's beliefs about the causes of illness to efforts to help children develop health-maintaining behaviors and cope with illness.

30.   Discuss how the concepts of *joint attention* and *social referencing* may show a dawning awareness in infants of mental states.

KEY TERMS

Upon completion of Chapter 7, you should be able to define the following terms.

Cognition _____

_____

Sensorimotor schemes _____

_____

Intentional behavior _____

_____

Representation _____

_____

Object permanence _____

_____

A-not-B error _____

_____

Progressive decentering_____

_____

Egocentrism _____

_____

Invariants _____

_____

Symbolic function _____

_____

Deferred imitation _____

_____

Symbolic play _____

_____

Qualitative identity _____

_____

Centration _____

_____

Conservation _____

_____

Class inclusion _____

_____

Seriation _____

_____

Transitivity _____

_____

Operations _____

_____

Reversibility_____

_____

Dual representation _____

_____

Hypothetical-deductive reasoning   _____

_____

Equilibration   _____

_____

Equilibrium _____

_____

Concept   _____

_____

Animism   _____

_____

Theory of mind _____

_____

False belief   _____

_____

Appearance–reality distinction   _____

_____

Joint attention   _____

_____

Social referencing   _____

_____

FILL-IN EXERCISES

Fill in the word or words that best fit in the spaces below.

1.   Piaget's goal throughout his career was to use the study of children to answer basic philosophical questions about the nature and origins of _____.

2.   For Piaget, the essence of intelligence does not lie in individually-learned responses or isolated memories; the essence lies in the underlying _____, which takes the form of various cognitive structures that the developing child constructs.

3.   _____ occurs through the complementary processes of assimilation and accommodation.

4.   The term _____ _____ refers to the skilled and generalizable action patterns by which infants act on and makes sense of the world. They are the cognitive structures of infancy.

5.   Substage 4 of the sensorimotor period is characterized by the emergence of the first truly _____ behavior.

6.   At substage 6 of the sensorimotor period, the infant becomes capable for the first time of mental _____.

7.   At _____ to _____ months the infant can search systematically and intelligently for hidden objects. The infant demonstrates object _____ by searching for an object, even when it is completely gone and even when it was not her own actions that made the object disappear.

8.   According to Piaget, the infant begins life in a state of profound _____; that is, he literally cannot distinguish between himself and the outer world.

9.   One general conclusion from later research is that Piaget often _____-estimated infants' knowledge.

10.   The defining characteristic of the movement from sensorimotor to preoperational intelligence is the onset of _____ ability, or what Piaget called the _____ function.

11.   Near the end of infancy, babies begin to imitate models observed some time in the past, an ability that Piaget referred to as _____ imitation.

12.   When retelling a story, young children often fail to assume the perspective of their listener, acting instead as though the listener already knows everything that they know. Such story telling demonstrates _____ speech by a preoperational child.

13.   The term _____ describes the preoperational child's tendency to focus on only one aspect of a problem at a time.

14.   Understanding that if A>B and B>C, then A>C involves the ability to appreciate the _____ of quantitative relations, an ability that develops in the _____ period.

15.   The term _____ refers to ability to order stimuli along some quantitative dimension, such as length.

16.   In the _____ operational period children are capable of mentally manipulating abstract as well as concrete objects, events, and ideas.

17.   The child who is concerned that a piece of paper will be hurt by being cut is displaying a form of reasoning that Piaget called _____.

18.   At about 1 year of age, babies engage in social _____: looking to another for cues about how to interpret and respond to an uncertain situation.

APPLICATION

Situation

Mickey and his older brother Dave are having lunch. When their mother gives them their juice, Mickey's glass is short and fat, while Dave's is tall and thin. Although their mother is careful to pour the same amount of juice into each glass, Mickey complains that Dave got more. Their mother gets a short, fat glass from the cupboard and, while Mickey watches, pours Dave's juice from the tall, thin glass into the new short, fat one. Mickey says "That's better, now they're the same." After watching his mother pour the juice from one glass into the other, Dave just sits there chuckling. He whispers to his mother, "Boy, did you ever fool Mickey! It's the same amount of juice in both glasses!"

Questions to answer

1.   Which of Piaget's stages of cognitive development most likely describes Mickey? How about Dave?

2.   What does Dave realize that Mickey doesn't? What is this concept called?

3.   According to Piaget's theory, what is it that causes Mickey to think there is more juice in the second glass? What is this process called?

USING WHAT YOU HAVE LEARNED

1.   Deanna is a very bright young girl. When her elementary school teacher gives her class an assignment, Deanna's work always turns out to be excellent. She finishes her work quickly, usually before anyone else in the class. This leaves Deanna with free time, which she often spends talking to and distracting other students who have not yet finished their work. Based on Piaget's findings regarding the motivation necessary for cognitive growth, what advice might you give Deanna's teacher if she asked you how to best to curb her disruptive behavior?

2.   A friend's mother claims that she was unable to program the video cassette recorder (VCR) to record a favorite program, until it was explained to her in terms of how she usually pre-programs the microwave to cook a chicken, while she is at work. How would you explain her success, in terms of the dual processes that make up the Piagetian concept of adaptation?

SAMPLE TEST QUESTIONS

1.   Piaget's research has shown a consistent focus on which of the following central topics of philosophy?

  a.   the child's understanding of space, time, and causality
  b.   the child's understanding of number and quantity
  c.   the child's understanding of classes and relations, invariance and change
  d.   all of the above

2.   The process by which we interpret the environment by altering our understanding to take account of new things is known as:

  a.   accommodation
  b.   adaptation
  c.   assimilation
  d.   organization

3.   Piaget's third period of cognitive development is called the:

  a.   preoperational period
  b.   concrete operational period
  c.   sensorimotor period
  d.   formal operational period

4.   At age 4, Derrick has a good understanding of the idea that poodles, German shepherds, bull terriers and rottweilers are all "dogs." When Derrick attends a birthday at a friend's house, he readily recognizes that his friend's cocker spaniel is also a dog. The process by which Derrick adapts to this new breed of dog best illustrates the Piagetian concept of:

    a. accommodation
    b. organization
    c. assimilation
    d. adaptation

5.   Which of the following is **NOT** viewed as a weakness in Piaget's studies of infants?

    a. The studies utilized only a limited sample of children, all of whom were from the same family.
    b. The method involved the longitudinal study of the behavior of the children as they developed in a natural setting.
    c. The method of study was carried out by two researchers both of whom were parents of the children involved.
    d. b & c

6.   In Piagetian theory, the first truly intentional behavior is characteristic of which substage of the sensorimotor period?

    a. Substage 2 (one to four months)
    b. Substage 3 (four to eight months)
    c. Substage 4 (eight to twelve months)
    d. Substage 5 (twelve to eighteen months)

7.   Sensorimotor schemes undergo which of the following developmental changes during the second substage (one to four months) of the sensorimotor period?

    a. Individual schemes become progressively refined.
    b. Individual schemes begin to be utilized more frequently in isolation.
    c. Initially independent schemes begin to be coordinated.
    d. a & c

8.   Baby Jacqueline spots her favorite toy rattle under her cat Ginger's tail. In order to retrieve her toy, Jacqueline needs first to lift the animal's tail before attempting to grasp the rattle. Jacqueline would be unable to perform this series of actions in which of the following substages of the sensorimotor period of development?

    a. Substage 3 (four to eight months)
    b. Substage 4 (eight to twelve months)
    c. Substage 5 (twelve to eighteen months)
    d. a & b

9.   According to Piagetian research, during the first two substages of the sensorimotor period, babies:

   a.   are able to solve problems only by means of trial and error
   b.   show essentially no evidence that they realize objects exist apart from their own actions on them
   c.   are unable, even after a number of trials, to anticipate the re-emergence of an object they have been tracking, once it disappears behind a screen
   d.   have developed a limited number of procedures for reproducing interesting events

10.   Ten-month-old Andrew and his baby-sitter are sitting on the floor playing with a stuffed rabbit. Andrew's baby-sitter has been hiding the rabbit behind her back, and each time she has done so, Andrew has crawled around behind her and retrieved the rabbit. To make the game more interesting, Andrew's baby-sitter next hides the toy behind a chair. When it is Andrew's turn to look for the toy, even though he watched it being hidden behind the chair, he continues to look for the rabbit behind her back. Andrew's behavior best illustrates Piaget's concept of:

   a.   A-not-B error
   b.   infant novelty and exploration
   c.   object permanence
   d.   infant egocentrism

11.   Piaget maintained that one important kind of knowledge that the child must acquire is a knowledge of what it is that stays the same. For Piaget, object permanence represented the first and most basic:

   a.   form of habituation
   b.   conservation task
   c.   cognitive invariant
   d.   form of adaptation

12.   In infancy, progressive decentering is manifest in:

   a.   an inability to distinguish the self from the outer world
   b.   a gradual distinguishing of self from the outer world
   c.   a tendency to focus on only one aspect of a problem at a time
   d.   a gradual willingness to share objects with others, and to engage in activities with others

13.   Which of the following is **NOT** an example of symbolic functioning in children?

   a.   A child opens her mouth prior to opening a jewelry box.
   b.   A child pretends that a plate is a flying saucer.
   c.   A child uses language.
   d.   A child sucks his thumb and the nipple of his milk bottle.

14.   Little Stacey loves playing peek-a-boo. Her favorite part is to cover her eyes with her hands and then call out "Nobody can see me!" Stacey is likely in which of Piaget's periods of cognitive development?

    a.   preoperational
    b.   formal operational
    c.   sensorimotor
    d.   concrete operational

15.   While spending a day at the beach with her family, Susan piles up and intricately decorates a large mass of sand. When Susan's father asks her what she is building, she tells him that it is the castle of a beautiful fairy princess. In Piagetian terms, Susan is engaging in:

    a.   assimilation
    b.   symbolic play
    c.   egocentrism
    d.   qualitative identity

16.   In Piaget's theory, knowledge that the quantitative properties of an object or a collection of objects are not changed by a change in appearance is an achievement of:

    a.   the sensorimotor period
    b.   the preoperational period
    c.   the concrete operational period
    d.   the formal operational period

17.   The term "animism" refers to the tendency of a child to:

    a.   endow inanimate objects with the qualities of life
    b.   confuse their perspective with that of others
    c.   are unable to focus on more than one aspect of a problem at a time
    d.   show confusion about how and why two events relate

18.   A child is presented with 13 flowers; 8 of these are red roses and 5 are white carnations. When asked whether there are more red roses or more flowers, a concrete operational child is likely to respond:

    a.   "there are more white flowers"
    b.   "there are more red roses"
    c.   "there are more white carnations"
    d.   "there are more flowers"

19.   "If Jane is older than Carol, and Carol is older than Christine, which girl is the youngest?" This type of question requires an understanding of:

a.   class inclusion
b.   conservation
c.   transitivity
d.   progressive decentering

20.   Piaget's theory of formal operations has been criticized on which of the following grounds?

a.   Critics have noted that the degree of within-stage consistency is not impressive.
b.   Critics have found that responses to different formal operational tasks are only moderately correlated.
c.   Logicians have criticized the specific logical structures that Piaget believed underlie formal operational performance.
d.   all of the above

ANSWERS

FILL-IN EXERCISES

1. knowledge   2. organization   3. adaptation   4. sensorimotor schemes   5. intentional
6. representation   7. eight; twelve; permanence   8. egocentrism   9. under   10. representational; symbolic
11. deferred   12 egocentric   13. centration   14. transitivity; concrete operations   15. seriation
16. formal   17. animism   18. referencing

APPLICATION

1. Mickey is preoperational. Dave is concrete or formal operational.
2. Dave realizes that the amount of juice remains the same. *Conservation*
3. Mickey focuses only on one aspect of the glass -- its height, and ignores the difference between the two glasses in width. *Centration*

SAMPLE TEST QUESTIONS

1. d	11. c
2. a	12. b
3. b	13. d
4. c	14. a
5. b	15. b
6. c	16. c
7. d	17. a
8. a	18. d
9. b	19. c
10. a	20. d

Chapter 8
Cognitive Development:
The Information-Processing Approach

OUTLINE

Use this outline as you read the chapter. Enter your questions, comments, and notes in the space provided. Write down terms or statements you don't understand, with their page numbers.

THE NATURE OF THE APPROACH

The Flowchart Metaphor

The Computer Metaphor

Comparisons with Piaget

MEMORY IN INFANCY

Recognition Memory

Recall Memory

MEMORY IN OLDER CHILDREN

The Role Of Strategies

Classics of Research
Watching Children Talk to Themselves: The Measurement of Mnemonic Strategies

The Role of Metamemory

The Role of Knowledge

Applications
Children's Eyewitness Testimony

NUMBER

Infants' Response to Number

Preschool Developments

Arithmetic

PROBLEM SOLVING

The Development of Rules

Reasoning by Analogy

The Contribution of Memory to Problem Solving

COGNITIVE CHANGE

Methods of Study

On the Cutting Edge
Using the Hands to Read the Mind

Mechanisms of Change

LEARNING OBJECTIVES

Upon completion of Chapter 8 you should be able to discuss the following topics. Check off those you are confident that you can discuss well. Re-read the material in the text for the topics about which you are less confident. Record the important points from your reading in the space below each topic.

1.   Explain how the flowchart metaphor is used by information-processing theorists.

2.   Describe how information-processing theorists have used the computer as a useful tool on a variety of levels.

3.   Compare and contrast the information-processing approach with the Piagetian approach.

4.   Differentiate between recognition memory and recall memory.

5.   Discuss how researchers have assessed recognition memory in infancy.

6.   Describe the developmental changes that have been found in recognition memory in infancy.

7.   Explain how researchers infer the presence of recall memory in infants.

8.   Discuss how the use of mnemonic strategies changes across age in childhood.

9. Differentiate between a utilization deficiency and a production deficiency in strategy use.

10. Discuss the two general reasons for psychologists' interest in metamemory.

11. Describe how constructive memory may be evident in children's recall.

12. Discuss the issues underlying children's eyewitness testimony.

13. Explain three ways in which expertise can affect memory.

14. Discuss how researchers have investigated infants' sensitivity to number.

15. Describe five principles that a counting system must honor, according to Rochel Gelman and associates. Do preschoolers understand these principles?

16. Discuss the various strategies that children might use to solve simple addition problems. How have Siegler and colleagues assessed these strategies?

17. Describe Robert Siegler's investigation of children's use of rules for solving the balance scale problem.

18.   Discuss two differences in how Siegler and Piaget account for conservation of number and of quantity in children.

19.   Explain what is meant by *analogical reasoning*. When is this form of reasoning first apparent?

20.   Discuss the roles of *operating space* and *short-term storage* space in Robbie Case's theory.

21.   Describe two possible explanations for the developmental increase in short-term storage capacity.

22.   Discuss five issues related to cognitive change for which Siegler believes microgenetic techniques can provide valuable data.

23.   How are self-modifying computer simulations used to study the process of cognitive change?

24.   Explain how *gesture-speech mismatches* may be related to cognitive change.

24.   Describe and differentiate among the following four mechanisms of cognitive change:

       Encoding

       Automatization

       Strategy construction

Strategy selection

25.   Discuss three challenges to the information-processing approach to cognitive development.

KEY TERMS

Upon completion of Chapter 8, you should be able to define the following terms.

Computer simulation   _____

_____

Recognition memory   _____

_____

Recall memory _____

_____

Reactivation   _____

_____

Infantile amnesia   _____

_____

Mnemonic strategies   _____

_____

Utilization deficiency   _____

_____

Production deficiency   _____

_____

Study strategies _____

_____

Metamemory _____

_____

Constructive memory _____

_____

Expertise _____

_____

Rules _____

_____

Executive function _____

_____

Analogical reasoning _____

_____

Operating space _____

_____

Short-term storage space _____

_____

Connectionism _____

_____

Gesture-speech mismatches _____

_____

Encoding _____

_____

Automatization _____

_____

Strategy construction _____

_____

Strategy selection _____

_____

FILL-IN EXERCISES

Fill in the word or words that best fit in the spaces below.

1. As compared to the stages of development proposed by Piaget, the stages proposed by information-processing theorists are more _____ specific.

2. The realization that some perceptually present stimulus or event has been encountered before is referred to as _____ memory.

3. A _____ strategy is any technique that people use to help themselves remember something.

4. The inability to remember experiences for the first 2 or 3 years of life is referred to as _____ _____.

5. The failure to generate a mnemonic strategy spontaneously is called _____ deficiency, whereas the failure of a recently developed strategy to facilitate recall is referred to as _____ deficiency.

6. The term _____ refers to knowledge about memory in general, and about one's own memory in particular.

7. Flavell coined the term _____ to refer to thinking about thinking.

8. The way in which people's general knowledge system structures and reworks the information they take in, and thus affects what they remember, is referred to as _____ _____.

9. Piagetian research makes the point that constructive memory can operate in a _____ as well as a _____ direction.

10.   The term _____ (sometimes called *content knowledge* or *knowledge base*) refers to organized factual knowledge with respect to some content domain.

11.   _____ reasoning refers to a form of problem solving in which the solution is achieved through recognition of the similarity between the new problem and some already-understood problem.

12.   According to Case, the total problem-solving resources available to a child are divided into two components, _____ space and short-term _____ space.

13.   The term _____ describes a theoretical and methodological approach adopted by many information-processing researchers that refers to self-modifying systems embodied in computer programs.

14.   Four major change mechanisms have been discussed by information-processing theorists. _____ refers to attending to and forming internal representations of certain features of the environment. _____ refers to an increase in the efficiency with which cognitive operations are executed as a result of practice. _____ _____ refers to the creation of strategies for processing and remembering information. _____ _____ refers to the progressively greater use of relatively effective, in comparison to relatively ineffective, strategies.

USING WHAT YOU HAVE LEARNED

1.   The text details the effects of constructive memory; it also presents research findings on the reliability of young children's eyewitness testimony. Based on your readings, how would you respond to a parent who is dismissing his child's claims of abuse as being attributable to a "vivid imagination."

2.   A friend mentions that crying is the only way her 4-month-old baby has of getting what she wants. The friend also mentions that the baby doesn't appear able to remember things, because as soon as a toy is removed from her sight, she forgets all about it. Using the mobile that hangs over the baby's crib, how could you show this mother that her baby is capable of doing more than crying to get what she wants? (Think in terms of having the baby act on the environment in order to obtain reinforcing consequences.) How might you also demonstrate the young infant's ability to remember?

3.   Not wanting your son to grow up with negative, stereotypical views about women, you tell him a bed-time story about a woman fire-fighter who is very strong and very brave. The next day you overhear him telling the same story to one of his stuffed animals, only this time, the fire-fighter in the story is a man. According to your knowledge of memory in children, how might you account for this change?

APPLICATION

Situation

Your 14-year-old brother is distressed and comes to you for advice. In two days he will be facing his final exam in Chemistry. He has read all 12 of the required textbook chapters over once, but doesn't "feel" like he knows very much.

Questions to Answer

1. Having read Chapter 8, you now have knowledge about the workings and limitations of memory. What suggestions would you make to your little brother to help him improve his study habits?

2. Based on what you know about mnemonic strategies, what could you tell your brother about note taking, outlining, organizing, and rehearsing the material he is studying?

3. What could you tell your brother about metamemory that might encourage him to go beyond a single reading of the textbook chapters to prepare for the exam?

4. How might information about the exam itself (e.g., that it consists of 100 multiple-choice questions) help you to be better able to suggest an optimal studying strategy to your brother? What would the implications of this information be in terms of recognition versus recall memory?

5. What would you tell your brother about some of the possible benefits of self-testing prior to the exam?

SAMPLE TEST QUESTIONS

1. Which of the following images is used to characterize the nature of the information-processing approach?

   a. a street map
   c. a balance scale
   b. a flowchart
   d. all of the above

2. One way information-processing theories differ from Piaget's theory is that

   a. Stages referred to in information-processing theories stages tend to be more domain-specific than those described by Piaget.
   b. Information-processing theorists are more concerned with cognitive development than was Piaget.
   c. Information-processing theorists are more concerned with a complex system of mental rules that underlie cognitive performance than Piaget.
   d. all of the above

3.   Infants, 12- to 24-months of age, were shown a series of pictures of various kinds of food, then given a choice of looking at either a previously-unseen item from the food category (e.g., an apple) or an item from a new category (e.g., a chair). What were the findings of this study?

    a.   The infants looked longer at the chair than the apple, thus demonstrating that they found a new category more interesting than a familiar one.
    b.   The infants looked longer at the apple than the chair, thus demonstrating a preference for the familiar category.
    c.   The infants spent an equal amount of time looking at each, thus demonstrating their inability to distinguish by category.
    d.   The amount of time spent looking at both the apple and the chair increased as a function of the age of the infant, thus demonstrating that a child's memory improves with development.

4.   Which of the following has been found effective in increasing the duration of memory in young infants?

    a.   providing an analogy
    b.   reactivation
    c.   providing simple rules
    d.   increasing short-term storage space

5.   Which of the following cannot be considered a possible explanation for infantile amnesia?

    a.   Infant memory systems differ qualitatively from later memory systems (e.g., nonverbal vs. verbal).
    b.   Infants lack a sense of self.
    c.   Infants do not form long-term memories.
    d.   Infants cannot share and rehearse memories within a social system.

6.   While his mother is out shopping, 12-year old Jeff receives a phone call. Although he writes nothing down, Jeff is able to relate the caller's request to his mother when she returns home a few hours later. In doing so, Jeff is using his:

    a.   metamemory   b.   recall memory
    c.   constructive memory   d.   recognition memory

7.   In one study, 3-year-olds played a memory game in which they had to keep track of a toy that had been hidden under one of several cups. Many children sat with their eyes glued to the critical cup and a finger planted firmly on it during the delay between hiding and retrieval. This act would be considered:

    a.   constructive memory   b.   elaboration
    c.   reactivation   d.   a rudimentary mnemonic strategy

8.   Research has found that children realize that familiar items are easier to remember than unfamiliar ones, that short lists are easier to learn than long ones, and that recognition is easier than recall. By what age does this realization generally exist in most children?

   a.   1 or 2 years   b.   3 or 4 years
   c.   5 or 6 years   d.   7 or 8 years

9.   When asked whether she thought it would be easier for her to remember a list of 3 items to buy at the store, or a list of 10 items, 8-year-old Janet answered that the list of 3 items would be easier to remember. This illustrates Janet's:

   a.   metamemory
   b.   compliance
   c.   recognition memory
   d.   recall memory

10.   When expertise in a particular area is high, memory in that area tends to be

   a.   low, because the child's storage space is cluttered with excessive detail.
   b.   unpredictable – you have to also consider the child's content knowledge and knowledge base.
   c.   unclear – expertise and memory are not related.
   d.   high – variations in expertise contribute to variations in memory.

11.   The role of "organized factual knowledge" is stressed in contemporary information-processing accounts of memory and problem solving. This term can be used interchangeably with which of the following terms?

   a.   content knowledge   b.   knowledge base
   c.   expertise   d.   all of the above

12.   In one study, children viewed pictures in which sex-stereotypic activities were reversed (e.g., a girl sawing and a boy playing with dolls). On a later memory test, the children tended to report that it was the boy who did the sawing, and the girl who played with dolls. This is an example of what type of memory?

   a.   constructive memory   b.   short-term memory
   c.   metamemory   d.   recall memory

13.   Infants response to number has been assessed using all of the following EXCEPT:

   a.   the habituation-dishabituation methodology
   b.   the possible-event, impossible-event procedure
   c.   conservation of quantity tasks
   d   ALL of the above have been used to assess infant response to number

14.   Children who follow Siegler's rule 4 on the balance scale problem:

    a.   Judge the task solely in terms of the number of weights on either side, when this number is different; if the number of weights is equal, however, they will also take distance into account.

    b.   Will be expected to solve the problem correctly in about 65% of trials, according to previous research.

    c.   Have mastered the weight-times-distance rule, realizing that downward force equals amount of weight multiplied by distance from the fulcrum.

    d.   Will, in Siegler's terms, have to "muddle through" in order to arrive at a solution for the problem.

15.   Which of the following is true concerning analogical reasoning?

    a.   The basic capacity for reasoning by analogy seems to be present early in life.

    b.   The ability to reason by analogy requires the abstract-reasoning abilities that emerge in adolescence.

    c.   Although analogical reasoning is evident in school-aged children, the basic capacity for this ability is not present in preschoolers.

    d.   Although some preschoolers may reason by analogy, such ability is beyond the capacity of infants.

16.   Children listened to a story in which a genie needed to transport some jewels over a wall and into a bottle. The genie solved her problem by rolling up a piece of posterboard to form a tube that she then rolled the jewels down into the bottle. The children then listened to a problem in which they were to help the Easter Bunny transport his eggs across a river and into a basket. Using aspects of the original story to solve the second problem involves:

    a.   constructive memory

    b.   reactivation

    c.   expertise

    d.   analogical reasoning

17.   According to Case's theory, short-term storage space:

    a.   can be increased through the use of mnemonic strategies

    b.   refers to the resources necessary to carry out whatever cognitive operations are being employed for the problem at hand

    c.   refers to the resources the child needs to store results from previous operations while carrying out new ones

    d.   all of the above

18.   In a conservation of volume task, three boys are each shown juice in a short, fat glass. The juice is then poured into a tall, thin glass, and each boy is asked whether the amount is the same as before. Which boy would be most likely to benefit from conservation training?

   a.   Davey, who says there is more juice because it is taller, and simultaneously signals his surprise by holding his hand over his mouth.
   b.   Billy, who while saying that there is more juice because it is taller, simultaneously gestures a change in width by cupping his hands
   c.   Stevie, who says there is more juice in the taller cup, and hits the table with his closed fist to make emphasize his point.
   d.   all of the above

19.   Which of the following is **NOT** a mechanism of cognitive change, discussed by information-processing theorists?

   a.   encoding
   b.   reactivation
   c.   automatization
   d.   strategy construction

20.   Which of the following is reasonably seen as a challenge to the information-processing theory of cognitive development?

   a.   the limited scope of the theory
   b.   the limited attention to the social context in which development occurs
   c.   the inability of the theory to produce a completely satisfactory explanation of how cognitive change occurs
   d.   all of the above

ANSWERS

FILL-IN EXERCISES

1. domain   2. recognition   3. mnemonic   4. infantile amnesia   5. production; utilization
6. metamemory   7. metacognition   8. constructive memory   9. negative; positive   10. expertise
11. analogical   12. operating; storage   13. connectionism   14. Encoding; Automatization;
Strategy construction; Strategy selection

SAMPLE TEST QUESTIONS

1. b	11. d
2. a	12. a
3. a	13. c
4. b	14. c
5. c	15. a
6. b	16. d
7. d	17. c
8. c	18. b
9. a	19. b
10. d	20. d

Chapter 9
Cognitive Development:
The Sociocultural Approach

OUTLINE

Use this outline as you read the chapter. Enter your questions, comments, and notes in the space provided. Write down terms or statements you don't understand, with their page numbers.

THE NATURE OF THE APPROACH

The Social Origins of Thought

On the Cutting Edge
Family Learning in Museums

Tools and Artifacts

The Cultural-Historical Study of Development

Comparisons with Cognitive-Developmental Theories

OBJECT EXPLORATION, TOOL USE, AND PLAY

Exploratory and Nonsymbolic Play

Symbolic Play

Implications of Symbolic Play for Development

MEMORY

Strategies

Event Memory

Autobiographical Memory

SELF-REGULATION

Planning

Private Speech

PEER INTERACTION AND COGNITIVE CHANGE

Peer Teaching

Collaboration

Peer Learning in Classrooms

Applications
Scaffolding Group Discussion: The Hypothesis-Experiment-Instruction Method

CULTURAL ARTIFACTS AND MATERIAL TOOLS

Numeration Systems

Measurement

Currency

LEARNING OBJECTIVES

Upon completion of Chapter 9 you should be able to discuss the following topics. Check off those you are confident that you can discuss well. Re-read the material in the text for the topics about which you are less confident. Record the important points from your reading in the space below each topic.

1.   Identify and describe three main themes in Vygotsky's writings

2.   Explain Vygotsky's notion of the *Zone of Proximal Development,* describing the relevance of *scaffolding* and *guided participation* to Vygotsky's notion?

3.   Describe how tools are related to higher mental functions.

4.   Identify and describe four interrelated time frames which Vygotsky proposed should be involved in the study of development.

5.   Discuss three differences between the sociocultural approach and the Piagetian and information-processing approaches to cognitive development.

6.   Discuss the importance of object play for children's cognitive development.

7.   Describe how cultures may differ in the access children are allowed to objects and in parental beliefs about object play.

8. Explain what *symbolic play* is, commenting on how it may be viewed differently by different cultures.

9. Describe how symbolic play with siblings differs from that with mothers.

10. Discuss how symbolic play may contribute to children's cognitive and social development.

11. Explain how the *school cut-off design* has been used to examine the effects of schooling on memory development.

12. Discuss what has been found concerning the influence of teachers and parents on memory strategies.

13. Describe how children's *scripts* and "memory talk" can influence their memory.

14. Identify two broad styles that parents use in talking about specific memories with children and explain how these influence children's *autobiographical memory*.

15. Discuss the ways in which children learn about and develop skills in planning.

16. Describe how the use of private speech develops in children.

17.   Discuss the practice of peer teaching, describing both the benefits of peer teaching, as well as the various reasons why child teachers may be insensitive to learners' needs.

18.   Contrast the sociocultural view of collaboration with that of Piaget.

19.   Describe the characteristics of successful collaborations.

20.   Describe the *hypothesis-experiment-instruction* intervention used to facilitate peer learning in Japanese classrooms.

21.   Explain how both the structure of the number-naming system, as well as the speed with which the number words can be pronounced, may contribute to the superior mathematical achievement of East Asian students.

22.   Describe how children's understanding of measurement develops

KEY TERMS

Upon completion of Chapter 9, you should be able to define the following terms.

Culture _____

_____

Zone of proximal development _____

_____

Scaffolding _____

_____

Guided participation _____

_____

Higher mental functions _____

_____

Ontogenetic development _____

_____

Microgenetic development _____

_____

Phylogenetic development _____

_____

Cultural/historical development _____

_____

Interdependent orientation _____

_____

Independent orientation _____

_____

Replica toys   _____

_____

Imaginary companions _____

_____

Solitary pretense   _____

_____

Sociodramatic play   _____

_____

Mediated memory   _____

_____

School cut-off design   _____

_____

Event Memory _____

_____

Script   _____

_____

Autobiographical memory   _____

_____

Private speech _____

_____

Sociogenesis _____

_____

Socio-cognitive conflict _____

_____

Intersubjectivity _____

_____

FILL-IN EXERCISES

Fill in the word or words that best fit in the spaces below.

1.   The term _____ refers to a method of teaching in which the adult adjusts the level of help provided in relation to the child's level of performance.

2.   Barbara Rogoff coined the term _____ _____ to describe the process by which young children become competent by participating in everyday, purposeful activities under the guidance of more experienced partners.

3.   According to Vygotsky, the term _____ refers to all the means individuals have at their disposal to achieve desired goals. The most powerful of these is _____.

4.   The Piagetian and information-processing approaches focus on processes _____ to the child, such as the reorganization of cognitive structures and increased speed of processing information. Sociocultural theorists, in contrast, believe developmental change is _____ mediated.

5.   Studies have shown that early experience exploring objects _____ (*may/may not*) be essential for normal cognitive development.

6.   As would be predicted by sociocultural theory, infants spend more time exploring objects and engage in more focused and complex exploration when interacting with _____ than when playing alone.

7.   Middle-income American culture is described as having a(n) _____ orientation, which emphasizes self-expression and personal achievement. Cultures such as Japan have a(n) _____ orientation that focuses on the individual's role within a broader social network.

8.   The most common type of joint pretense, _____ _____, occurs when two or more people enact a variety of related roles (e.g., mother and baby; driver and passenger).

9.   Observational studies reveal that most pretend play takes place in a _____ context with other people acting as spectators or partners.

10.   Observations in European American homes suggest that children's earliest play partner is most often _____.

11.   Children _____ (*with/without*) siblings are twice as likely to demonstrate knowledge of false beliefs than those _____ (*with/without*) siblings.

12.   _____ memory involves remembering that relies on cultural tools and artifacts that support memory development and use.

13.   The _____ _____-_____ design is a research design that compares children who are close in age, but differ in school experience by one year.

14.   A _____ is a representation of the typical sequence of actions and events in some familiar context. They increase in both completeness and _____ as children develop.

15.   The term _____ _____ refers to memories that are specific, personal, and long-lasting – memories that are part of one's life-history and that have to do with the self.

16.   Researchers have identified two broad styles that parents use to elicit talk about specific memories with young children. Parents in the _____ category provide richer narrative structure than parents in the _____ category.

17.   Vygotsky referred to the process of acquiring knowledge or skills through social interactions as _____.

18.   In their attempts to scaffold others' learning, peer teachers tend more frequently to provide too _____ (*little/much*) assistance.

19.   Studies show that children begin to learn by watching peers at least by the _____ year of life.

20.   Piagetians refer to the conflict that arises during social interaction as _____ _____.

21.   From the sociocultural approach to collaboration, it matters less that partners hold divergent views on a problem than that they establish _____ -- a commitment to find common ground on which to build shared understanding.

22.   In the Japanese educational intervention known as _____-_____-_____, the teacher provides three or four plausible alternatives. Students then choose one of these choices as correct, and their choices are discussed with the other students in class.

23.   The Oksapmin of Papua New Guinea use what is called a _____-_____ _____ system for counting and measuring.

24.   Research on children's measurement demonstrates the general point that children can often use tools skillfully _____ (*before/after*) they really understand them.

USING WHAT YOU HAVE LEARNED

You've been asked by the parent-teacher association of your neighborhood school to give a short talk on collaboration in the classroom. They ask you to talk about the following issues. What would you say?

1.   Is collaboration really that valuable?

2.   What do children learn through the process of collaboration?

3.   At what age can collaboration be introduced in school?

4.   Is it better to have friends, or classmates who are simply acquaintances, work together?

5.   Is it better to put together children who have the same understanding of a problem, or children who differ in their level of understanding?

6.   What role should the teacher play in collaborative groups?

APPLICATION

Do you use self-guiding, private speech?

In Chapter 9, you read about the role of private speech in the control of behavior, and how private speech becomes internalized as thought as children become older. You also learned that self-guiding private speech can be seen even in older children, when they begin a new and difficult task, with its use decreasing as they master the task.

1.   Pay close attention to your own "internalized" private speech. Can you see evidence of its self-guiding functions?

2.   Try doing an unfamiliar and complicated task (such as a puzzle, Rubik's cube, etc.). Pay close attention to your own verbalizations and self-statements. Do you see evidence of private speech?

3.   Think of a complicated task that you recently learned, such as driving. Do you remember initially guiding your behavior through the use of private speech (e.g., "OK, now, shift into drive." "Watch that car over there!" "Got the turn-signal on?"). Did your use of private speech decline as you became more familiar with the task? Are there any situations (such as the stress of a near accident while driving) where your private speech re-emerges? *

---

* To learn more about private speech and these examples read Meichenbaum, D. (1977). *Cognitive-Behavior Modification*. Plenum Press: New York.

SAMPLE TEST QUESTIONS

1.   Vygotsky used the term "zone of proximal development" to describe:

    a.   the distance between what a child can accomplish independently and what he/she can accomplish with the help of an adult

    b.   a method of teaching in which the adult adjusts the level of help provided to the child's level of performance, the goal being to encourage independent performance

    c.   the process by which young children become competent by participating in everyday, purposeful activities under the guidance of more experienced partners

    d.   all of the above

2.   Which of the following themes in Vygotsky's writings have proved especially influential in guiding contemporary sociocultural theory and research?

    a.   Individual mental development has its origins in social sources.

    b.   Human thought and action are mediated by cultural tools.

    c.   The study of mental functioning requires the study of change across multiple levels.

    d.   All of the above

3.   Vygotsky proposed the study of development over four interrelated time frames. Development across years of an individual's life, such as childhood, is referred to as:

    a.   phylogenetic development

    b.   microgenetic development

    c.   ontogenetic development

    d.   cultural/historical development

4.   How does the sociocultural view of development differ from the view of Piaget?

    a.   Sociocultural approaches focus on processes within the individual child, such as the reorganization of cognitive structures.

    b.   Sociocultural theories view cognitive development as changes in internal mental capabilities.

    c.   Sociocultural theorists do not believe that there are universal stages in children's cognitive development.

    d.   Sociocultural theorists focus on speed of processing information.

5.   Some scholars believe that different socialization practices are rooted in cultural conceptions of the self. Cultures that focus on the self's role within a broader social network, emphasizing interpersonal connectedness, social obligation, and conformity, are described as having a(n) _____ orientation.

    a.   interpersonal   b.   interdependent

    c.   interconnected   d   collaborative

6.   Rebecca loves to play doctor and patient with her mother. Rebecca pretends to be the doctor, and her mother pretends to be sick or have an injury. This type of activity is referred to as

    a.   solitary pretense
    b.   sociodramatic play
    c.   solitary pretense with imaginary companions
    d.   interdependent pretense

7.   In which of the following would we expect to see more advanced play in a toddler?

    a.   Little Sarah plays alone with her stuffed animals, giving names to each.
    b.   Little Colleen plays with her two imaginary companions, "Stephie" and "Princess Mary."
    c.   Little Jennifer plays alone with replica toys that resemble real objects in a house.
    d   Little Francine plays dolls with her mother as play partner.

8.   Which of the following questions would a 4-year-old be better able to answer?

    a.   What happened yesterday?
    b.   What happened last week?
    c.   What happens at birthday parties?
    d.   What happened at Billy's birthday party yesterday?

9.   Which of the following parental styles of talking with children is more likely to improve children's autobiographical memory?

    a.   the elaborative style   b.   the deliberative style
    c.   the attentive style   d.   the repetitive style

10.   Which of the following is true concerning children's private speech?

    a.   Private speech decreases when children are in the presence of responsive social partners.
    b.   Private speech occurs most often on impossibly difficult tasks.
    c.   Children with learning and behavior problems tend to rely on private speech for a longer time than their peers.
    d.   All of the above are true.

11.   Billy, who is 8 years old, is attempting to teach his classmate Dave how to solve a classification problem. What level of assistance is he most likely to offer?

    a.   Just the right amount, since the two boys are close in age.
    b.   Too little assistance.
    c.   No assistance, since Dave is likely engaged in private speech.
    d.   Too much assistance.

12.   Which of the following explanations may account for the relatively poor ability of children to scaffold the learning of other children?

a.   Children may lack the self-regulatory skills to step back and let their partner solve the problem.
b.   Children may lack the social-cognitive skills required for effective teaching.
c.   The multiple demands of both solving the problem and teaching the solution to someone else may overwhelm child teachers.
d.   All of the above

13.   Piaget laid out three conditions necessary for cognitive change to occur when partners are collaborating. Which of the following is NOT one of those conditions?

a.   Cognitive change occurs best when partners share a common language and system of ideas.
b.   Cognitive change occurs best when one or both partners are unsure about their point of view, so that they can be influenced by the other partner.
c.   Cognitive change occurs best when there is reciprocity between partners so that each feels free to express his or her own point of view.
d.   Actually, all of the above **ARE** conditions Piaget felt were necessary for change to occur.

14.   The sociocultural approach differs from the Piagetian account of collaboration in its view of cognitive change as resulting from

a.   cooperation and coordination   b.   conflict and resolution
c.   competence and motivation   d.   argument and reconciliation

15.   One important difference between the sociocultural approach to collaboration and the Piagetian view is that

a.   Piaget felt that even preoperational-aged children could effectively collaborate, whereas socioculturalist feel that only older children can collaborate effectively.
b.   Piaget felt that children could not collaborate effectively until the period of concrete operations, whereas socioculturalists believe young children can collaborate effectively.
c.   Piaget felt that collaboration was not important for children's social-cognitive development, whereas the socioculturalists feel that it is.
d.   Piaget felt that collaboration was important for children's social-cognitive development, whereas the socioculturalists feel that it is not.

16.   Which of the following factors is associated with productive collaboration?

a.   collaboration characterized by lively discussion and debate
b.   collaborating with strangers or acquaintances
c.   collaborations where neither partner has an advanced understanding of the problem
d.   all of the above

17.   Which of the following variables is necessary for successful whole-class instruction?

a.   Students need to come to school prepared to view their teachers as the authority.
b.   Students need to come to school prepared to teach their peers.
c.   Students need to feel comfortable making mistakes and revealing confusions in public.
d.   All of the above

18.   Which of the following is NOT a factor that may contribute to the superior mathematical achievement of East Asian students over U.S. students?

a.   In East Asian languages, the structure of the base-10 number system is clearly represented by the structure of the number names themselves.
b.   East Asian children have larger memory spans that American children.
c.   In East Asian languages, the number names can be pronounces more quickly than in English.
d.   All of the above

19.   In industrialized societies, children initially

a.   pay little attention to the size of measuring units, focusing instead on the number of units counted
b.   pay little attention to the number of units counted, focusing instead on the size of the measuring units
c.   pay attention to both size and number of units
d.   focus first on size, then on number of units

20.   Five-year-old Suzie is asked by her teacher to draw her own ruler and then to use it to measure. Based on what we know about children's measurement, what is Suzie most likely to do?

a.   place the numbers haphazardly on the ruler, showing no sense of order or counting
b.   show no understanding of where to begin numbering, starting with the number 3 or 4
c.   place the number 1 in correspondence with the first line on the ruler
d.   become confused between metric and English units of measurement

ANSWERS

FILL-IN EXERCISES

1. scaffolding 2. guided instruction 3. tools; language 4. internal; socially 5. may not
6. caregivers 7. independent; interdependent   8. sociodramatic play 9. social
10. the mother 11. with; without 12. mediated 13. school cut-off 14. script; complexity
15. autobiographical memory 16. elaborative; repetitive 17. sociogenesis 18. much
19. second 20. sociocognitive conflict 21. intersubjectivity 22. hypothesis-experiment-instruction
23. body-part enumeration 24. before

SAMPLE TEST QUESTIONS

1. a	11. d	
2. d	12. d	
3. c	13. b	
4. c	14. a	
5. b	15. b	
6. b	16. a	
7. d	17. c	
8. c	18. b	
9. a	19. a	
10. c	20. c	

Chapter 10
Intelligence and Schooling

OUTLINE

Use this outline as you read the chapter. Enter your questions, comments, and notes in the space provided. Write down terms or statements you don't understand, with their page numbers.

THE NATURE OF IQ TESTS

The Binet Approach to Measuring Intelligence

Other Tests of Childhood Intelligence

Evaluating the Tests

ISSUES IN THE STUDY OF INTELLIGENCE

Organization of Intelligence

Stability of IQ

Origins of Individual Differences

CONTRIBUTIONS OF THE FAMILY

Longitudinal Studies

Research with the HOME

Cross-Cultural Studies

SCHOOLING: VARIATIONS AND EFFECTS

Cross-Cultural Studies

Classics of Research
An Early Study of the Effects of Schooling on Thinking

Amount of Schooling

Quality of Schooling

Contextual Contributors to Schooling

SCHOOLING: EXPERIMENTAL INTERVENTIONS

An Illustrative Intervention Project

Project Head Start

Overview

Race and Intelligence

On the Cutting Edge
Stereotype Threat

ALTERNATIVE CONCEPTIONS OF INTELLIGENCE

Evolutionary Approaches

Applications
Approaches to Teaching Literacy

Dynamic Testing

Gardner's Multiple Intelligences

Giftedness and Creativity

LEARNING OBJECTIVES

Upon completion of Chapter 10 you should be able to discuss the following topics. Check off those you are confident that you can discuss well. Re-read the material in the text for the topics about which you are less confident. Record the important points from your reading in the space below each topic.

1.   Summarize the important differences between the psychometric approach and the Piagetian, information-processing, and sociocultural perspectives.

2.   Describe the origin and content of the Stanford-Binet intelligence test.

3.   Describe the two Wechsler tests designed to assess childhood intelligence (the WISC-III and the WPPSI) and explain how they differ from the Stanford-Binet.

4.   Describe the advantages of the Kaufman Assessment Battery for Children (K-ABC).

5.   Distinguish between the concepts of test reliability and validity.

6.   Describe the relationship between IQ and academic performance.

7. Discuss the "general versus specific" question concerning the organization of intelligence.

8. Discuss the relationship between infant intelligence and later intelligence. How may "response to novelty" link intelligence in infancy and childhood?

9. Summarize two rules for predicting the stability of IQ across childhood.

10. Summarize the general findings of family studies, adoption studies, and twin studies concerning the origins of individual differences in intelligence.

11. Explain the concept of *heritability*. What are the limitations of the heritability statistic?

12. Describe the HOME instrument and discuss the findings of research using it .

13. Discuss how differences in mothers' expectations may account for cultural differences in children's academic achievement.

14. Discuss how schooling may affect cognitive development.

15. Explain how amount of schooling is related to IQ. Is there evidence for a cause-effect direction to this relationship?

16.   Differentiate factors that do and do not influence school success, as identified in the research of Michael Rutter.

17.   Discuss the pros and cons of the practice of *ability grouping*.

18.   Discuss two general kinds of evidence that support Eccles' argument that typical middle school or junior high provides a poor *stage-environment* fit for young adolescents.

19.   Explain the importance of peers, parents, and general cultural background to success at school.

20.   Describe the Abecadarian Project and Project Head Start. What are the similarities and differences between these projects?

21.   Outline three major conclusions about the possibility of modifying intelligence by changing the environment that can be drawn from the results of intervention projects like the Abecadarian Project and Project Head Start.

22.   Explain the basis of the IQ-race controversy and summarize three arguments against the position that there are genetically-based IQ differences between races.

23.   Describe how *stereotype threat* can affect academic performance and explain how researchers have attempted to alleviate its effects.

24.   Explain how evolutionary psychologists conceptualize intelligence, differentiating between *biologically primary abilities* and *biologically secondary abilities*.

25.   Explain how the tasks of understanding and teaching reading have been conceptualized by each of the following four theoretical approaches:

evolutionary and biological approaches

environmental/learning approaches

cognitive-developmental approaches

sociocultural approaches

26.   Explain what *dynamic assessment* refers to, discussing how such procedures differ from traditional IQ assessments.

27.   Discuss how Howard Gardner's theory of multiple intelligences differs from more traditional approaches to intelligence. What are the 8 distinct intelligences proposed by Gardner?

28.   Discuss the relationship between IQ and giftedness. What characteristics other than high IQ characterize gifted children?

29.   Contrast *convergent thinking* and *divergent thinking*. How do these styles of thinking relate to creativity?

KEY TERMS

Upon completion of Chapter 10, you should be able to define the following terms.

Psychometric _____

_____

Reliability _____

_____

Validity _____

_____

g _____

_____

Hierarchical model of intelligence _____

_____

Heritability _____

_____

Flynn effect _____

_____

HOME _____

_____

Ability grouping _____

_____

Stage-environment fit _____

_____

Cultural compatibility hypothesis _____

_____

Stereotype threat   _____

_____

Environment of evolutionary adaptiveness _____

_____

Biologically primary abilities   _____

_____

Biologically secondary abilities   _____

_____

Phonological awareness_____

_____

Dialogic reading_____

_____

Reciprocal teaching   _____

_____

Dynamic assessment   _____

_____

Convergent thinking   _____

_____

Divergent thinking   _____

_____

FILL-IN EXERCISES

Fill in the word or words that best fit in the spaces below.

1. The first successful intelligence test was developed in Paris in 1905 by Alfred _____ and Theodore _____.

2. The ability to predict _____ success was the prime criterion for an item's inclusion in the first intelligence test.

3. The Stanford-Binet is a global measure of intelligence, designed to yield a single "_____ _____," or IQ score, that summarizes a child's ability.

4. There is no absolute metric for measuring intelligence, such as there is for measuring height or weight. Instead, a child's IQ is a function of how that child's performance _____ with the performance of other children the same age.

5. The accuracy with which a measuring instrument assesses the attribute that it is designed to measure is referred to as its _____.

6. To determine the structure of intelligence, psychometric researchers use a statistical procedure called _____ _____ to make sense of the pattern of correlations across different measures of intelligence.

7. Spearman proposed a two-factor theory of intelligence: factor _____ refers to general intelligence, while _____ refers to abilities that contribute to performance on particular tasks.

8. A number of researchers have suggested that the common thread linking intelligence in infancy to intelligence in childhood may be an individual's response to _____.

9. The Fagan Test of Infant Intelligence measures how long infants look at _____ as compared to _____ pictures.

10. Results of adoption studies reveal that typically the adopted child's IQ correlates more strongly with the IQs of the _____ parents than with the IQs of the _____ parents.

11. The most widely accepted contemporary estimates of the heritability of IQ place the value at _____ to _____.

12. The _____ Effect refers to an increase over time in the average level of performance on IQ tests.

13. _____ _____ is the practice of separating students into groups of similar ability for purposes of instruction.

14. According to the notion of _____-_____ fit, development proceeds most smoothly when then environmental opportunities and challenges during a particular time period match the capacities and needs of the developing child.

15. Children who have participated in intervention programs typically have higher IQs than children who have not; these effects show a tendency to _____ with time.

16. _____ _____ refers to the extra pressure people feel in situations in which their performance may confirm a negative stereotype held about their group.

17. Geary uses the term biologically _____ abilities to refer to abilities shaped by natural selection to solve recurring problems faced by ancestral humans.

18. Children's knowledge of the internal sound structure of spoken words is called _____ _____.

19. _____ _____ is a form of joint picture-book reading in which the adult uses open-ended questions and other prompts to encourage the child to tell the story, with the goal of promoting linguistic skills.

20. _____ teaching is an instructional procedure in which children learn to monitor their understanding of text by observing and imitating strategies of predicting, clarifying, questioning, and summarizing.

21. Studies using the _____ _____ procedure have confirmed Vygotsky's claim that IQ tests provide an incomplete picture of children's intelligence.

22. Howard Gardner argues that humans possess at least _____ relatively distinct intelligences.

23. _____ thinking is right-answer-oriented thinking – the form of thought emphasized on IQ tests.

24. Most contemporary accounts of creativity can be labeled _____ theories, on that they stress the coming together of multiple contributors that must work together to make creativity possible.

APPLICATION

Situation

Andrea and Mark have just experienced the delivery of their first child -- a baby boy. After a standard period of maternity leave, Andrea will be returning to her full-time job as a chemist. Since Mark is required to work long hours at his accounting firm, the couple have arranged for a baby-sitter to come into their home, during the day, once Andrea returns to work. Still, the couple is very concerned about baby Alex's intellectual development. From their past experience with friends who have children, it seems that the children of stay-at-home mothers develop more quickly, and end up being the most competent performers at school. This leads them to suspect that the amount of time parents spend with their children is a critical factor in children's intellectual development.

Questions to Answer

1. Based on your knowledge of research on the home environment as a context within which a child's intellectual skills develop, is there any evidence to suggest that the total amount of time spent with a child is a critical determinant of a child's intellectual development?

2. What suggestions might you make to Andrea and Mark in order for them to create a home environment that will be maximally beneficial to Alex's intellectual development? What role can they play in determining the kinds of experiences he has, even when they're not interacting with him?

3. What recommendations would you make to Andrea and Mark concerning how they should interact with Alex when they are with him?

4. Upon checking with the baby-sitter, Andrea learns that Alex is quite happy to play with one or two favorite toys in his play pen most of the day. The baby-sitter is generally pleased to leave him there, because if he were allowed to wander freely he might break something.   How should Andrea respond?

5. Being first-time parents, Andrea and Mark are uncertain about the extent that they will eventually need to discipline Alex. From your reading of Chapter 10 concerning the relation between parental discipline and children's IQ, what would you suggest to these parents?

USING WHAT YOU HAVE LEARNED

1. A researcher investigating the heritability of IQ in a sample of 15 year-old Hawaiian children finds the heritability in this sample to be .60. What expectations would this finding impose if the same researcher later investigated the heritability of IQ in a sample of French-speaking Canadian children of the same age?

2. You are discussing the relatively-poor mathematics performance of American children as compared to the that of children from China and Japan. A friend asserts that the blame for this difference rests squarely on the American school system. How would you respond?

3. You see on an afternoon television talk show an "expert" commenting on the issue of racial differences in IQ. This individual argues that differences between African Americans and White Americans are genetic in origin. Whose research is this "expert" likely to present to support this position? A second expert then presents a countervailing position. What evidence would this second expert present to counter the first expert's genetic position?

SAMPLE TEST QUESTIONS

1. The Stanford-Binet test of intelligence:

    a. is a direct historical descendant of the original Binet-Simon test
    b. has been revised several times since it was first developed in 1916
    c. is a test of childhood intelligence, that is applicable to every age group within the span of childhood, except infancy
    d. all of the above

2. Which of the following general abilities is the current version of the Stanford-Binet intelligence test **NOT** intended to assess?

    a. long-term memory
    b. verbal reasoning
    c. quantitative reasoning
    d. fluid reasoning

3. One difference between the Wechsler tests and the Stanford-Binet is that:

    a. the Wechsler tests include an explicit attempt at cultural diversity and cultural fairness
    b. the Wechsler tests have a grounding in information-processing conceptions of intelligence
    c. the Wechsler tests measure sequential processing as well as simultaneous processing
    d. the Wechsler tests are divided into a verbal and a performance scale

4.   Louis Thurstone argued for a differentiated model of intelligence. The intelligence test he developed was designed to assess how many "primary mental abilities?"

a.   1   b.   6   c.   7   d.   2

5.   In the earliest attempts to predict later intelligence from scores on infancy IQ tests, the first conclusion was that traditional tests of infant intelligence:

a.   did not relate well to later intelligence test scores
b.   related very well to later intelligence test scores
c.   related to later intelligence test scores partially for female subjects, but not at all for males
d.   were not of any use at all

6.   One of the main findings to emerge from adoption studies concerns the pattern of correlations in parent/child IQ. Typically, the adopted child's IQ:

a.   correlates more strongly with the IQs of the adoptive parents than with the IQ of the biological parents
b.   correlates more strongly with the IQ of the biological parents than with the IQs of the adoptive parents
c.   does not correlate with the IQ of the biological parents in cases where the child was adopted shortly after at birth
d.   correlates more strongly with the IQ of the adoptive mother than of the adoptive father

7.   A researcher studying children who have been adopted at birth finds that in her sample of 100 adopted children the majority have above-average IQs, falling in the 105 to 110 range. What is likely the most plausible explanation for this finding?

a.   Adoptive parents tend to be highly-motivated parents, and adoptive homes tend to be privileged in various ways.
b.   By chance, this researcher happened to test a sample of children with an average IQ that was unusually high compared to that of the population as a whole.
c.   Children who are adopted tend to work extremely hard in school, and stay in school longer than children who are not adopted. This contributes to their acquisition of the specific skills and the specific kinds of knowledge that IQ tests measure.
d.   All of the above are equally plausible explanations for this finding.

8.   The term "heritability" refers to:

a.   the proportion of variance in a trait that can be attributed to genetic variance in the sample being studied
b.   the degree to which an adopted child's IQ correlates with the IQs of his adoptive parents
c.   an estimate of the extent to which differences among people come from differences in their genes as opposed to differences in their environments
d.   both a & c

9.   Which of the following is supported by studies using the HOME instrument?

     a.   There is a strong genetic component to intelligence.
     b.   The quality of the child's home environment is predictive of later IQ.
     c.   Home environments are related to IQ for boys but not for girls.
     d.   Home environments are related only to certain aspects of intelligence.

10.   Which of the following is a true statement, according to the results of the Stevenson group's study?

     a.   American mothers were more likely than Asian mothers to regard effort as more important for school success than ability.
     b.   American mothers were more likely to provide outside-of-school help for their children's academic endeavors than were Chinese or Japanese mothers.
     c.   Asian mothers were more likely than American mothers to regard effort as more important to school success than ability.
     d.   American mothers were the LEAST satisfied with the school performance of their children, which fell well below the academic achievement of the Chinese and Japanese children.

11.   Schools as well as homes can affect children's intellectual development. Cross-cultural studies indicate that schooling promotes which of the following cognitive skills?

     a.   classification
     b.   metacognition
     c.   memory
     d.   all of the above

12.   On which of the following tasks would you expect Joanne, who has been to school, to outperform Rheta, who has not?

     a.   recognizing that a piece of play-dough that is rolled into a big, round ball, and one that is rolled out into a long, skinny string, actually have the same mass
     b.   remembering a list of 10 items to buy at the store by repeating the list of items to herself over and over again
     c.   realizing that a half-cup of water maintains the same volume, whether it is left in a large, shallow bowl, or poured into a tall, narrow wine glass
     d.   all of the above

13.   It has long been known that there is a positive relation between number of years of education completed and IQ score. In explaining this, Stephen Ceci has argued that:

     a.   schooling may actually increase IQ
     b.   IQ tests are over-rated as predictors of school performance
     c.   IQ tests are not valid measures of intelligence
     d.   IQ tests do not predict school performance

14.   Participation in an early intervention program is generally associated with:

    a.   higher scores on standardized achievement tests
    b.   lower probability of being assigned to special education classes
    c.   lower probability of being retained in a grade
    d.   all of the above

15.   Which of the following is **NOT** a documented positive effect of participation in the well-known intervention program, Project Head-Start?

    a.   greater success in school
    b.   improvements in children's IQs lasting until adolescence
    c.   better health status
    d.   a and b

16.   Reciprocal teaching:

    a.   allows teachers more free time, because students take over and teach one another
    b.   provides the opportunity for older, more experienced teachers to share their skills with newer, less experienced teachers
    c.   allows children the opportunity to observe and imitate strategies of predicting, clarifying, questioning, and summarizing
    d.   is a novel teaching technique in which students teach one another in a "teacherless" class

17.   The early emergence of _____ is a good predictor of eventual reading abilities.

    a.   dialogic reading
    b.   phonological awareness
    c.   spatial intelligence
    d.   convergent thinking

18.   Howard Gardner's approach to intelligence emphasizes:

    a.   application of g to many contexts of human behavior
    b.   the use of factor analysis to determine the structure of intelligence
    c.   distinct, multiple intelligences accounting for ability in different domains
    d.   the primary importance of linguistic intelligence

19.   According to Geary's evolutionary approach, skills such as reading and higher mathematics are called:

    a.   biologically secondary abilities   b.   biologically-based abilities
    c.   biologically prized abilities   d.   biologically inherited abilities

20.   When asked what she could use a newspaper for, Sarah says: "Well, you could read it. Then, you could make paper dolls out of it. You could also roll it up and use it like a vase to put flowers in. You could also use it like wallpaper to decorate your room. You could put it under your coat to keep warm. You can also use it for hamster litter. You could even cut it into small pieces and put it in the garden soil to help fertilize your plants." Sarah's thinking would be described as:

    a.   means-ends thinking
    b.   inappropriate thinking
    c.   divergent thinking
    d   dynamic thinking

ANSWERS

FILL-IN EXERCISES

1. Binet, Simon   2. academic   3. intelligence quotient   4. compares   5. validity   6. factor analysis
7. *g; s*   8. novelty   9. novel; familiar   10. biological; adoptive   11. .4 to .7   12. Flynn
13. ability grouping   14. stage-environment   15. diminish   16. stereotype threat   17. primary
18. phonological awareness   19. dialogic reading   20. reciprocal   21. dynamic assessment   22. eight
23. convergent   24. confluence

SAMPLE TEST QUESTIONS

1. d	11. d
2. a	12. b
3. d	13. a
4. c	14. d
5. a	15. b
6. b	16. c
7. a	17. b
8. d	18. c
9. b	19. a
10. c	20. c

Chapter 11
Language Development

OUTLINE

Use this outline as you read the chapter. Enter your questions, comments, and notes in the space provided. Write down terms or statements you don't understand, with their page numbers.

THEORIES OF LANGUAGE DEVELOPMENT

Nativistic Theory

Environmental/Learning Approaches

Cognitive-Developmental Models

Sociocultural Approaches

THE PREVERBAL PERIOD

Speech Perception

Listening Preferences

Early Sounds

Gestures and Nonverbal Responses

Transition to Words

SEMANTICS

Early Lexical Development

Mechanisms of Semantic Development

GRAMMAR

Development of Grammar

On the Cutting Edge
Shared Language Data: The CHILDES System

Classics of Research
Adding Endings to "Wugs" and Things

Mechanisms of Grammar Acquisition

On the Cutting Edge
Is Language Separate from General Cognitive Ability? The Message from Williams Syndrome

PRAGMATICS

Speech Acts

Discourse

Social Referential Communication

Applications
Language Differences in School: Teaching (and Learning) One Language or Two?

LEARNING OBJECTIVES

Upon completion of Chapter 11 you should be able to discuss the following topics. Check off those you are confident that you can discuss well. Re-read the material in the text for the topics about which you are less confident. Record the important points from your reading in the space below each topic.

1.   Discuss the basic principles of the following four theoretical approaches to language acquisition:

Nativistic

Environmental/learning

Cognitive-developmental

Sociocultural

2.   Describe preverbal receptive language abilities and preferences in infants.

3.   Outline and discuss the importance of the development of expressive language abilities in infants (i.e., early sounds and gestures).

4.   Describe deficits in the language development of deaf babies.

5.   Explain the differences between a *referential style* and an *expressive style* of lexical development. How do biology and environment interact to produce these two styles?

6.   Describe the nature of children's early words, focusing on the following characteristics of early word use:

overextensions

underextensions

coining

holophrases

7. Explain how grammatical cues contribute to semantic development. Why is this process called *syntactic bootstrapping*?

8. Explain how *lexical contrast theory* and the *principle of mutual exclusivity* act as constraints permitting children to acquire the meanings of new words quickly.

9. Discuss how parents contribute to children's semantic development.

10. Describe the development of grammar as children move from single-word to more sentence-like communications.

11. Explain why the CHILDES has been valuable for language development researchers.

12. Explain what *overregularization* involves. Differentiate this term from the term *overextension*, discussed earlier.

13. Explain what is meant by *semantic bootstrapping*. Differentiate this term from *syntactic bootstrapping*, discussed earlier.

14.   Describe how the notion of *operating principles* explains grammar acquisition.

15.   Describe the strategies for acquiring grammar proposed by *competition model*.

16.   Discuss the role parents play in grammar acquisition. Is *motherese* important? Explain each of the following parental responses: expansions, recasts, and clarification questions.

17.   Discuss how Williams syndrome may provide evidence for the nativistic view of language.

18.   Explain what is meant by "rules of discourse," and how such rules are important for conversation.

19.   Discuss how speaker skills and listener skills are important for social referential communication.

20.   Discuss the one- versus two-language hypotheses concerning how bilingual children approach the task of learning two languages.

KEY TERMS

Upon completion of Chapter 11, you should be able to define the following terms.

Productivity   _____

_____

Nativistic theory _____

_____

Surface structure _____

_____

Deep structure _____

_____

Language acquisition device (LAD) _____

_____

Transformational grammar _____

_____

Motherese _____

_____

Language acquisition support system (LASS) _____

_____

Phonology _____

_____

Phoneme _____

_____

Categorical perception _____

_____

Cooing _____

_____

Reduplicated babbling _____

_____

Babbling drift _____

_____

Semantics _____

_____

Lexicon _____

_____

Naming explosion _____

_____

Referential style_____

_____

Expressive style _____

_____

Overextension _____

_____

Underextension_____

_____

Coining _____

_____

Holophrase _____

_____

Syntactic bootstrapping _____

_____

Fast-mapping _____

_____

Constraints _____

_____

Lexical contrast theory _____

_____

Principle of mutual exclusivity _____

_____

Grammar _____

_____

Syntax _____

_____

Inflections _____

_____

CHILDES (Child Language Data Support System) _____

_____

Telegraphic speech _____

_____

Overregularization _____

_____

Semantic bootstrapping _____

_____

Operating principle   _____

_____

Language-making capacity (LMC)   _____

_____

Competition model   _____

_____

Expansion   _____

_____

Recast _____

_____

Clarification question   _____

_____

Pragmatics   _____

_____

Speech act   _____

_____

Discourse   _____

_____

Social referential communication   _____

_____

FILL-IN EXERCISES

Fill in the word or words that best fit in the spaces below.

1. Chomsky's psycholinguistic model proposes that the brain contains a speech-analyzing mechanism, referred to as the _____ _____ _____.

2. Structured social interactions or "routines" taking place between infants and their mothers, that are central to the language acquisition support system, are referred to as _____.

3. The term _____ refers to contrasts in speech sounds that change the meaning of what is heard.

4. By _____ _____ of age, infants seem to lose a good deal of their ability to discriminate sound contrasts to which they have not been exposed.

5. At about 2 months of age, infants begin to produce one-syllable vowel sounds known as _____.

6. At about _____ months of age, reduplicated babbling occurs.

7. Infants first begin to use gestural responses for communication at about _____ to _____ months of age.

8. Gestures in infants may serve a referential communication function. Initially, this form of behavior involves _____, where babies hold up objects for an adult's acknowledgment. These gestures may then evolve into _____, and eventually into _____ and _____.

9. By the age of 18 months, average children possess a lexicon of about _____ spoken words, and about _____ words that they understand.

10. Children who display a _____ style produce a large proportion of nouns and object labels, whereas those who display a _____ style place a greater emphasis on language as a pragmatic tool for expressing needs and for social interaction.

11. Overextensions and underextensions both characterize word learning. Although less common in production, _____ are frequent in comprehension.

12. When confronted with an object for which they do not know the name, children sometimes overextend the label of a similar object. Alternatively, they may deal with gaps in their vocabulary by creating new words, a process called _____.

13. A _____ is a single word sentence used to express a larger idea. It is common during the second year of life.

14. Children as young as 3 can sometimes acquire at least a partial meaning of a word after only one exposure to it, a process called _____-_____.

15.   According to _____ _____ theory, when children hear an unfamiliar word they automatically assume the new word has a different meaning from that of any word they already know.

16.   The principle of _____ _____ states that children believe that objects can only have one name.

17.   _____ are certain endings added to words that modify the meanings of words.

18.   The aspect of grammar that involves word order is referred to as _____.

19.   When children apply the rules to every noun or verb, including exceptions, they make an error known as _____.

20.   _____ _____ refers to a proposed mechanism of grammatical development in which children use semantic cues to infer aspects of grammar.

21.   Slobin developed a model of the child's language-making capacity (LMC) that includes more than 40 _____ principles.

22.   Repeating a child's incorrect statement in a corrected or more complete form is referred to as _____, whereas restating the child's remark using a different structure is called _____.

23.   The belief that children continually strive to find better ways of communicating their needs or desires has led to the study of the social uses of language, referred to as _____.

24.   Social _____ communication is a form of communication in which a speaker sends a message in such a way that the listener understands it.

APPLICATION

Try to get a chance to observe people talking with young children. Pay close attention to "how" they talk.

1.   Can you see signs of motherese in their speech? What characteristics of motherese do you see?

2.   Is motherese only used by mothers? Do fathers use it? How about other children?

3.   If you have the opportunity, try to observe people who differ in how accustomed they are to interacting with young children. Are there differences in how they talk to children? Does using motherese seem related to a person's familiarity with young children?

4.   Some skeptics argue that there is nothing special about the way adults talk to young children. They argue that motherese can be seen in other interactions, even those that don't involve talking to children. Can you see evidence of such non-child motherese (e.g., pet owners talking to dogs, children talking to toys)? Why would people use such a style of talking? Is this necessarily evidence against the notion of motherese?

USING WHAT YOU HAVE LEARNED

People who are unfamiliar with normal language development often misinterpret the normal phases of language development that children go through as a sign either that a child is extremely advanced linguistically, or of a problem in the child's language development. Below are some examples of how some parents might misinterpret the language of their children. From what you have read in Chapter 11, identify what language phenomenon the parent is actually describing, and think about how you would correct the parent's misconception.

1. "I think I may have a genius on my hands! Little Billy is only six months old, and already he's said his first word. Yesterday he said 'da-da.' To think his first word was daddy! Today he didn't get it quite right, he said 'da-da-da,' but I'm sure that was just a mistake. Just think, his first word at six months!"

2. "Kim seems to be losing what she had. She used to say things correctly, but now she makes all kinds of mistakes. Like, just yesterday she said 'I breaked it,' when she used to say 'broke.' The other day she said 'my foots' when she used to say 'my feet.' I wonder if the other kids at the day care are a bad influence on her?"

3. "I'm not sure what's wrong with little Nancy. She can't tell the difference between a dog, a cat, and even a squirrel. She calls cats and squirrels 'doggie.' I'm worried she may have some kind of vision problem."

4. "Little Billy sure has some weird ideas. Yesterday we went to the pet store and looked at the fish. He has a goldfish at home. When I told him that these sure were pretty fish at the pet store, he said 'No!, Them not fish, fish at home!' Does he really think he's the only one who has a fish?"

5. "Carol doesn't seem to want to learn new words. All she does is use words she already has. The other day, she saw a kiwi-fruit and instead of asking what it was, she said 'that's the fuzzy-egg.' Will she ever learn any new words?"

SAMPLE TEST QUESTIONS

1.   Chomsky's views of language acquisition challenged _____ theory, a theory that previously had been generally accepted by psychologists.

    a.   Bandura's
    b.   Bruner's
    c.   Piaget's
    d.   Skinner's

2   "Surface structure" refers to:

    a.   a hypothetical structure, located on the surface of the brain, that analyzes speech input
    b.   inborn knowledge humans have about the properties of any language system
    c.   the structured context that parents provide for language learning
    d.   the way words and phrases are arranged in spoken languages

3   The language acquisition support system (LASS) is an important concept in which view of language acquisition?

    a.   psycholinguistic
    b.   sociocultural
    c.   cognitive-developmental
    d.   ethological

4.   The notion that children use their early cognitive concepts to extract rules of language from the speech they hear is associated with which approach to language acquisition?

    a.   psycholinguistic
    b.   cognitive-developmental
    c.   learning-based approach
    d.   socio-cultural

5.   "Cooing" consists of:

    a.   identical sounds, strung together
    b.   gestures and nonverbal responses
    c.   a single word used to express a larger idea
    d.   one-syllable vowel sounds

6.   At around six months of age, babies begin to string together several identical sounds, to produce what is described as:

    a.   cooing   b.   reduplicated babbling
    c.   holophrases   d.   telegraphic speech

7. The hypothesis that the sounds infants make while babbling become increasingly similar to those they are hearing in the language around them is known as:

    a. babbling drift
    b. reduplicated babbling
    c. naming explosion
    d. referential style

8. Infants begin to use gestures as a form of referential communication at around:

    a. 4-5 months of age
    b. 6-7 months of age
    c. 8-9 months of age
    d. 11-12 months of age

9. Which of the following is **NOT** a form of referential communication involving gestures?

    a. requesting
    b. pointing
    c. labeling
    d. showing

10. Some children produce a very large proportion of nouns, especially object names, and use language primarily to label things. This style is referred to as:

    a. expressive
    b. referential
    c. overextensive
    d. expansive

11. A child points to a rake and says "that's the grass-comb." This is an example of:

    a. overextension
    b. expansion
    c. coining
    d. overregularization

12. Little Sarah says "Ball!" and points to her favorite ball. Her parents have figured out that when she says this, she is expressing the entire sentence "I want the ball!" This is an example of:

    a. a holophrase
    b. an operating principle
    c. telegraphic speech
    d. an overextension

13.   Little Phil was given a silver dollar by his grandfather. He calls it "cookie." This is an example of:

    a.   coining
    b.   overregularization
    c.   overextension
    d.   underextension

14.   Little Manal told her mom "I brushed my teeths, mommy, because I eated too much candies." This sentence contains examples of:

    a.   coining
    b.   overregularization
    c.   telegraphic speech
    d.   overextension

15.   Two-year-old Gail has a pet poodle. The other day, her uncle said "That's a nice poodle you have there, Gail." Little Gail began crying, and said "Not poodle, him dog!" Gail's response is best explained by the:

    a.   semantic bootstrapping explanation
    b.   competition model
    c.   lexical contrast theory
    d.   principle of mutual exclusivity

16.   The grammar in little Gail's statement in question 11 illustrates:

    a.   a holophrase
    b.   overregularization
    c.   telegraphic speech
    d.   an operating principle

17.   Which of the following is **NOT** a characteristic of "motherese?"

    a.   short utterances spoken slowly
    b.   frequent grammatical errors
    c.   repetition and frequent labeling
    d.   focus on the here-and-now

18.   When mothers respond to their children's ill-formed statements by repeating the incorrect statement in a corrected or more complete form, this form of feedback is referred to as:

    a.   recasting
    b.   a clarification question
    c.   expansion
    d.   selective imitation

19.   The belief that children acquire language because it provides them with a powerful tool for communicating with others and achieving their goals is characteristic of which approach?

a.   sociocultural approach
b.   cognitive-developmental approach
c.   nativist approach
d.   social-learning approach

20.   Which of the following is **NOT** true about bilingual children?

a.   Bilingual children have been found to be more advanced than monolinguals in some areas of cognition.
b.   Younger bilingual children frequently mix or combine forms of the two languages within the same utterance.
c.   Children in bilingual homes initially acquire both languages more slowly than children in monolingual homes.
d.   Having to simultaneously learn two languages results in cognitive deficits associated with the slower growth of language skills.

Answers

Fill-in Exercises

1. language acquisition device   2. formats   3. phoneme   4. one year   5. cooing   6. six   7. eight, ten
8. showing; giving; pointing, labeling   9. 50; 100   10. referential; expressive   11. underextensions
12. coining   13. holophrase   14. fast-mapping   15. lexical contrast   16. mutual exclusivity   17. Inflections
18. syntax   19. overregularization   20. semantic bootstrapping   21. operating   22. expansion; recasting
23. pragmatics   24. referential

Using What You Have Learned

1. reduplicated babbling   2. overregularization   3. overextension   4. underextension   5. coining

Sample Test Questions

1. d	11. c
2. d	12. a
3. b	13. c
4. b	14. b
5. d	15. d
6. b	16. c
7. a	17. b
8. d	18. c
9. a	19. a
10. b	20. d

Chapter 12
Early Social and Emotional Development

OUTLINE

Use this outline as you read the chapter. Enter your questions, comments, and notes in the space provided. Write down terms or statements you don't understand, with their page numbers.

THEORIES OF EARLY SOCIAL DEVELOPMENT

Evolutionary and Biological Approaches

Environmental/Learning Approaches

Cognitive-Developmental Approaches

Sociocultural Approaches

MUTUAL REGULATION BETWEEN INFANTS AND CAREGIVERS

Crying

Emotions and the Affective System

Face-to-Face Interactions

TEMPERAMENT

Defining Temperament

Conceptualizing Temperament

Temperament and Social Interactions

Temperament and Behavior Problems

ATTACHMENT

Developmental Course of Attachment

Assessing Attachment

Determinants of Attachment

Classics of Research
Mother Love: Harlow's Studies of Attachment

Consequences of Attachment

EFFECTS OF EARLY EXPERIENCE

Effects of Early Daycare

Applications
Child-Caregiver Sensitivity and Attachment

Effects of Trauma

Effects of Abuse

Effects of Childhood Hospitalization

LEARNING OBJECTIVES

Upon completion of Chapter 12 you should be able to discuss the following topics. Check off those you are confident that you can discuss well. Re-read the material in the text for the topics about which you are less confident. Record the important points from your reading in the space below each topic.

1.   Outline the major arguments of each of the following four major theoretical approaches to attachment:

evolutionary and biological

environmental/learning

cognitive-developmental

sociocultural

2.   Briefly describe two conditions necessary for us to conclude that crying serves as a form of communication.

3.   Briefly describe the development and expression of emotions in infancy, and discuss the role of the social environment in emotional development.

4.   Describe the development of infants' ability to recognize emotions.

5.   Briefly describe the importance of newborn cycles to mother-infant interaction.

6.   Discuss how mother-infant *turn-taking* may show cultural variations.

7.   Explain why premature infants may be at greater risk for being abused than are full-term babies, with reference to mother-infant interaction.

8.   Present three important questions that have guided attempts to define temperament.

9.   Describe the major characteristics of the following three behavioral styles identified by Thomas and Chess of the New York Longitudinal Project:

The *easy* baby

The *difficult* baby

The *slow-to-warm-up* baby

10.   Identify and describe the major characteristics of the dimensions of temperament comprising the EAS model.

11.   Discuss the two areas of individual temperamental differences described by Rothbart.

12.   Briefly discuss three explanations for the finding that *difficult* babies display more behavior problems in early childhood.

13.   Explain what is meant by the term *inhibition* and discuss the relevance of this characteristic to shyness in children.

14.   Outline and describe the three phases of the development of attachment.

15.   Briefly outline the key components of the Strange Situation procedure.

16.   Describe the Strange-Situation behavior of infants displaying each of the four patterns of attachment.

17.   Describe the AQS method for assessing attachment.

18.   Discuss how patterns of attachment may be related to culture.

19.   Briefly discuss how maternal responsiveness and infant temperament are related to attachment.

20.   Describe the four attachment styles underlying mothers' descriptions of their own childhood attachment relations using the Adult Attachment Interview.

21.   Describe the cognitive and social consequences of secure attachment.

22.   Discuss the findings of studies examining the effects of early day care and attachment.

23.   Describe the characteristics of *post-traumatic stress disorder* (PTSD) in children. What types of situations are most often associated with PTSD?

24.   Briefly discuss how infant abuse and neglect and attachment are related.

KEY TERMS

Upon completion of Chapter 12, you should be able to define the following terms.

Primary caregiver   _____

_____

Socialization   _____

_____

Social Cognition_____

_____

Internal working model   _____

_____

Emotion   _____

_____

Affect   _____

_____

Display rules   _____

_____

Social referencing   _____

_____

Microanalysis   _____

_____

Interactional synchrony _____

_____

Affect Mirroring _____

_____

Temperament _____

_____

Goodness of Fit _____

_____

New York Longitudinal Study (NYLS) _____

_____

EAS model _____

_____

Inhibition _____

_____

Maternal bonding _____

_____

Wariness of strangers _____

_____

Separation protest _____

_____

Strange situation procedure _____

_____

Attachment Q-Set (AQS) _____

_____

Adult attachment interview _____

_____

FILL-IN EXERCISES

Fill in the word or words that best fit in the spaces below.

1.   The term _____ refers to the process through which society molds the child's beliefs, expectations, and behavior.

2.   Children's and adults' knowledge of human behavior and social interactions is referred to as _____ _____.

3.   Some theorists believe that infants and caregivers develop *internal* _____ _____ of each other that they then use to interpret events and predict how others will behave towards them.

4.   Smiling, reflecting pleasure, appears in response to the human voice or a moving face at around _____ or _____ weeks of age.

5.   _____ _____ are the expectations and attitudes a society holds toward the expression of affect.

6.   When the mother comes to recognize the baby's cycles of attention and inattention, and adjusts her behavior to these cycles, mother and baby develop an *interactional* _____ in behavior.

7.   *Affect* _____ refers to the degree to which caregivers gauge their communicative behaviors to respond to input from their infants.

8.   The New York Longitudinal Study identified three early behavioral styles: the _____ baby, the _____, baby, and the _____ baby.

9.   According to the EAS model, temperament can be measured along three dimensions. _____ refers to how quickly the baby becomes aroused; _____ describes the baby's tempo; and _____ refers to the baby's preference for being with other people. A fourth component, _____, refers to the child's response to unfamiliar people.

10. Rothbart views temperament as consisting of individual differences in two areas: _____ and _____.

11.   Jerome Kagan's research reveals that children who are quick to respond negatively to an unfamiliar situation may be displaying a temperamental trait called _____.

12.   Some researchers believe that skin-to-skin contact during a sensitive period immediately after birth is important for the development of _____ _____.

13.   Three general phases of attachment can be described. In Phase 1, infants display _____ social responsiveness. In Phase 2, they display _____ social responsiveness. In Phase 3, they display _____ attachment.

14.   Mary Ainsworth classified mother-infant attachment into three categories. Pattern B infants are considered _____ attached; pattern A infants are called insecure- _____; pattern C infants are called insecure- _____. More decently, a fourth category (pattern D), labeled insecure _____, has been identified.

15.   Harlow's research demonstrated that the most significant factor in attachment is not the opportunity for feeding, but the opportunity to cling and snuggle, a phenomenon he called _____ comfort.

16.   Researchers using the Adult Attachment Interview report the following: _____ mothers claim to have difficulty recalling and appear to assign little significance to their childhood; _____ mothers tend to dwell on their early experiences; _____ mothers have experienced attachment-related trauma that they have not yet dealt with, and _____ mothers present an objective and balanced picture of their childhood.

17.   _____ _____ disorder is a disorder in which a particularly stressful event results in later emotional symptoms, including reexperiencing the event, increased responsiveness to the outside world, a tendency to be easily startled, and nightmares.

18.   Parental maltreatment (overstimulation and understimulation) seems related to attachment: _____ has been linked to insecure-resistant attachment (pattern C), while _____ has been linked to the insecure-avoidant (pattern A) pattern of attachment.

APPLICATION

Freud felt that the mother-infant relationship is the first love relationship experienced by an individual, and that the attachment relationship forms the basis for all later love relations experienced by the infant. Other theorists also believe that secure or insecure attachment in infancy may set the stage for secure or insecure romantic relationships in adulthood.

1.   Does the notion that attachment in infancy may affect later love relations make sense to you?

2.   How could you go about researching this possible relationship? What type of design would you use?

3.   Suppose you do, indeed, find that people who developed an insecure attachment with their caregivers in infancy have difficulty forming close relationships with others as adults. Is it necessarily true that the difficulties they have with their adult relationships are **because** of their insecure attachment in infancy? Can you think of any other possible explanation (e.g., the role of temperament)?

USING WHAT YOU HAVE LEARNED

In Chapter 12, you read about the importance of caregiver - infant attachment, and about characteristics of caregivers that can either foster or hinder development of a secure attachment. You also read about the controversy over working mothers and infant day care. Suppose that a friend of yours is a new mother. She wants to return to work, but is agonizing over the decision to place her infant in day care. She is particularly concerned with choosing the "right" day care.

1.   What would you advise her to look for in a day care?

2.   What characteristics in the day care workers should she look for?

3.   She worries the baby will become attached to the day care worker rather than her. Is she right? Will the baby become attached to the day care worker? Would that mean it cannot develop a secure attachment to her?

SAMPLE TEST QUESTIONS

1.   The notion that the process of natural selection has provided infants and mothers with innate behaviors designed to ensure the infant's survival, is attributable to:

    a.   Jerome Kagan   b.   John Bowlby
    c.   Mary Rothbart   d.   Robert Plomin

2.   Which of the following is characteristic of the ethological approach to early social development?

    a.   Babies develop internal working models of their caregivers and themselves that they use to interpret events.
    b.   When they encounter an unfamiliar person or situation, babies respond with uncertainty to the discrepancy between the situation and their representations of how things typically are.
    c.   Mother-infant social behaviors result from interaction between the two individuals, with each influencing the behavior of the other.
    d.   The mother's job is to "read" the infant's signals and decide what is wrong, what she should do, and when it is effective.

3.   According to environmental/learning approaches, how should an infant respond if its mother does not respond to its smiling and vocalizations?

    a.   It will develop an internal working model of its mother as unresponsive, which will interfere with the development of attachment.
    b.   It will perceive this reaction as discrepant from its cognitive representation for its mother's typical behavior, and will react with uncertainty.
    c.   It will decrease, or perhaps stop its smiling and vocalization.
    d.   It will try to motivate the mother to provide adequate caregiving by crying.

4.   Smiling to indicate pleasure first appears:

    a.   immediately after birth
    b.   during the first week
    c.   after 10 to 12 weeks
    d.   after 5 or 6 months

5.   Little Billy got his finger caught in the door. Although it wasn't seriously injured, it really hurt. He tried hard to hold back the tears, because he knows that "big boys don't cry." His attempt not to cry shows his understanding of his culture's

    a.   level of affect mirroring
    b.   emotional display rules
    c.   internal working models
    d.   expectations about social referencing

6.   Social referencing refers to:

a.   the way in which the mother comes to recognize and adjust her behavior with reference to the infant's cycles of attention and inattention
b.   the process of comparing a social situation to a schema that the infant has developed for similar situations
c.   the expectations an infant develops with reference to its caregiver's social behavior
d.   the infant's use of cues from its caregivers to determine how to react when he or she encounters an unfamiliar object or person

7.   Which of the following is **NOT** one of the three behavioral styles identified by Thomas and Chess?

a.   the difficult baby
b.   the hard-to-slow-down baby
c.   the slow-to-warm-up baby
d.   the easy baby

8.   Little Ricky's eating and feeding schedules are not very predictable. He cries often, seldom seems to be in a good mood, and reacts intensely to changes in his environment. Which of Thomas and Chess's behavioral styles would best describe Ricky?

a.   the difficult baby
b.   the hard-to-slow-down baby
c.   the slow-to-warm-up baby
d.   the easy baby

9.   Of babies that can be classified according to the Thomas and Chess typology, the smallest percentage are described as:

a.   easy
b.   slow-to-warm-up
c.   hard-to-slow-down
d.   difficult

10.   The "A" in Plomin's EAS model of temperament refers to:

a.   the infant's preference for being with other people
b.   how quickly a baby becomes aroused by and responds negatively to stimulation from the environment
c.   the baby's tempo and energy use
d.   the adaptability of the baby to changing situations

11.   Rothbart's "Reactivity" is similar to Plomin's dimension of:

a.   Emotionality
b.   Activity
c.   Sociability
d.   Melancholy

12.   Kagan and his colleagues describe a temperamental response style, called _____, in which infants react to unfamiliar people and situations with timidity, shyness, and fearfulness.

    a.   sociability
    b.   inhibition
    c.   insecure-avoidant
    d.   emotional reactivity

13.   Some researchers believe that maternal bonding takes place during a sensitive period occurring

    a.   immediately after birth
    b.   throughout the first 2 months of life
    c.   across the first year of life
    d.   across the first two years of life

14.   Behaviors indicating that the infant has formed an attachment with its primary caregiver can be observed:

    a.   in the first few hours after birth
    b.   during the first 2 months of age
    c.   at around 3 months of age
    d.   at around 8 months of age

15.   Mary Ainsworth's typology of attachment consists of all of the following, except:

    a.   insecure-inhibited   b.   insecure-avoidant
    c.   securely-attached   d.   insecure-resistant

16.   Babies who react to the Strange Situation with distress when the mother leaves, but respond enthusiastically when she returns, are classified as:

    a.   insecure-inhibited
    b.   insecure-avoidant
    c.   securely-attached
    d.   insecure-resistant

17.   When exposed to the Strange Situation, little Carol was distressed, even when her mother was there. She was especially upset when her mother left. When her mother returned, although Carol was relieved, she also seemed angry with her mother. Carol's attachment would be classified as:

    a.   insecure-inhibited
    b.   insecure-resistant
    c.   insecure-avoidant
    d.   securely-attached

18.   Which of the following is unlikely to be associated with secure attachment?

a.   delaying responding to the infants' crying, in order to not "spoil" the baby
b.   feeding the baby at a comfortable pace
c.   affectionate and tender handling of the infant
d.   Actually, ALL of the above ARE associated with secure attachment

19.   In response to the Adult Attachment Interview, *unresolved* mothers

a.   claim to have difficulty recalling their childhoods, appearing to assign little significance to them
b.   tend to dwell on early experiences that they describe in a confused and emotional manner
c.   have experienced attachment-related trauma that they have not yet dealt with
d.   none of the above

20.   Studies have found that, in comparison to Pattern A or C infants, Pattern B infants tend later to be:

a.   better problem solvers
b.   more socially competent
c.   less likely to develop emotional or behavior problems
d.   all of the above

ANSWERS

FILL-IN EXERCISES

1. socialization 2. social cognition 3. working models 4. ten, twelve   5. display rules   6. synchrony
7. mirroring 8. easy, difficult, slow-to-warm-up 9. emotionality; activity; sociability; shyness
10. reactivity; self-regulation   11. inhibition   12. maternal bonding   13. indiscriminate; discriminate;
focused   14. securely; avoidant; resistant; disorganized/disoriented   15. contact   16. dismissing;
preoccupied; unresolved; autonomous   17. posttraumatic stress   18. understimulation; overstimulation

SAMPLE TEST QUESTIONS

1. b	11. a
2. d	12. b
3. c	13. a
4. c	14. d
5. b	15. a
6. d	16. c
7. b	17. b
8. a	18. a
9. d	19. c
10. c	20. d

Chapter 13
Development of the Self

OUTLINE

Use this outline as you read the chapter. Enter your questions, comments, and notes in the space provided. Write down terms or statements you don't understand, with their page numbers.

THEORIES OF THE SELF

Cognitive-Developmental Approaches

Environmental/Learning Approaches

Evolutionary and Biological Approaches

Classics of Research
Monkey in the Mirror: Primate Self-Recognition

Sociocultural Approaches

SELF-KNOWLEDGE

Discovery of the Self in Infancy

Self-Recognition

Developmental Changes in Self-Descriptions

On the Cutting Edge
Globalization and the "Cultural Self": Are We All Bicultural Now?

SELF-EVALUATION

Measuring Self-Esteem

The Developmental Progression of Self-Esteem

Gender Differences in Self-Esteem

Academic Self-Concept

Applications
Possible Selves and Academic Achievement

SELF-REGULATION

The Emergence of Self-Control

Compliance

Resistance to Temptation

Delay of Gratification

LEARNING OBJECTIVES

Upon completion of Chapter 13 you should be able to discuss the following topics. Check off those you are confident that you can discuss well. Re-read the material in the text for the topics about which you are less confident. Record the important points from your reading in the space below each topic.

1.   Explain what is meant by each of the following components of the self-system: *self-knowledge*, *self-evaluation*, and *self-regulation*.

2.   Describe how self-schemas influence how children understand and relate to the world around them.

3.   Outline the five stages of Selman's model of children's awareness of the self.

4.   Explain how Bandura explained the development of self-evaluation and of self-regulation in children.

5.   Describe how infant-caregiver interactions lead to the development of a sense of self, according to Bowlby's theory.

6.   Explain three questions about the self that have interested evolutionary psychologists.

7.   Explain how cultural practices influence the shaping of the self.

8.   Discuss the processes involved in the infant's development of an initial sense of separateness and of personal agency in his or her world.

9.   Describe how researchers use visual self-recognition to infer the development of self-knowledge in infants.

10.   Discuss how temperamental and attachment differences may affect self-recognition in infants.

11.   Contrast children's self-descriptions at three Piagetian stages of cognitive development.

12.   Briefly describe Harter's and Marsh's procedures for assessing self-esteem in children.

13. Describe three factors that may account for a decrease in self-esteem as children approach adolescence.

14. Describe how boys and girls differ in self-esteem.

15. Discuss age and gender differences in academic self-concept.

16. Contrast how children who display a *mastery-oriented* pattern and those who display a *helpless* pattern respond to failure experiences.

17. Contrast the beliefs of children who hold an entity model with those who hold an incremental model of intelligence. How are these views related to the mastery-oriented and helpless patterns?

18. Discuss how the praise and criticism can affect children's academic self-concept.

19. Explain how children's social comparisons may affect their self-evaluations of competence, and how such comparisons change across grade level.

20. Describe how children's academic self-concept may be influenced by their parents' expectations of their abilities.

21. Describe children's progression from external control to self-control.

22. Contrast *committed compliance* with *situational compliance*.

23. Explain how researchers assess children's resistance to temptation and discuss the factors that influence children's behavior in such situations.

24. Describe the delay-of-gratification technique. Discuss the factors that have been found to affect children's ability to delay gratification.

KEY TERMS

Upon completion of Chapter 13, you should be able to define the following terms.

Existential self _____

_____

Categorical self _____

_____

Self-system _____

_____

Self-knowledge (self-awareness) _____

_____

Self-evaluation _____

_____

Self-regulation _____

_____

Self-schema _____

_____

Self-efficacy _____

_____

Evaluative self-reactions _____

_____

Personal agency _____

_____

Visual self-recognition _____

_____

False self behavior _____

_____

Self-esteem (self-worth) _____

_____

Looking-glass self _____

_____

Competence _____

_____

Self-consciousness _____

_____

Academic self-concept _____

_____

Entity model _____

_____

Incremental model _____

_____

Social comparison _____

_____

Possible selves _____

_____

Compliance _____

_____

Committed compliance _____

_____

Situational compliance _____

_____

Forbidden toy technique _____

_____

Delay of gratification technique _____

_____

FILL-IN EXERCISES

Fill in the word or words that best fit in the spaces below.

1. The "I," or _____ self is the subjective experience of the world whereas the "Me," or _____ self is an objective entity seen and evaluated in the world.

2. Self-_____ is the part of the self-system concerned with what children know about themselves. Self-_____ is the part of the self-system concerned with children's opinions of themselves and their abilities. Self-_____ is the part of the self-system that is concerned with self-control.

3. Selman's model is most concerned with children's self-_____.

4. Self-_____ are constructed over time and serve primarily to organize self-related information.

5. A person's view of his/her own ability to carry out various behaviors is referred to by Bandura as the person's self-_____.

6. Evaluative _____-_____ is Bandura's term for consequences people apply to themselves as a result of meeting or failing to meet their personal standards.

7. Along with infants' knowledge that they exist apart from the things around them comes an understanding of _____ _____; that is, an understanding that they can be the causes of events in their world.

8. _____ _____ describes the play of two preverbal children with similar toys in a similar fashion, involving coordinated action. This type of play involves some degree of self- and other-awareness.

9. As babies approach age 2, many display an increasing awareness of self through their use of pronouns such as _____ and _____.

10. Babies do not recognize their image in a mirror before about _____ months, and self-recognition does not occur reliably until about _____ months.

11. By _____ years of age, many children display knowledge of some of their most basic characteristics, such as whether they are girls or boys, and that they are children rather than adults.

12. Adolescents can display _____ _____ behavior, meaning that, when necessary, they can behave in ways that do not reflect their true selves.

13. According to the idea of the _____-_____ self, the psychological portraits we paint of ourselves are based on how we think others see us.

14.   Many investigators report that at about age 11 or 12, children's self-_____ tends frequently to decrease, only to increase again over the subsequent years.

15.   Typically, children's academic self-concept is highest in _____, but declines across the next four grades.

16.   According to Dweck's model, _____-oriented children view failure experiences as an opportunity to learn from their experiences, whereas _____ children avoid future challenges, because they view failure as a sign of low self-worth.

17.   In terms of their theories of intelligence, some children believe in a(n) _____ model, in which the amount of a person's intelligence is fixed and unchangeable, whereas others believe in a(n) _____ model, in which a person's intelligence can grow with experience and learning.

18.   Children with _____ *(lower/ higher)* opinions of their academic competence tend also to make fewer social comparisons.

19.   _____ *(fathers/mothers)* of children with high academic self-concept have been found to be warmer and more supportive in their interactions than those of children with low academic self-concept.

20.   _____ _____ is the term used to refer to concepts of the self in the future that represent one's goals, dreams, hopes, and fears.

21.   _____ compliance results when the child embraces the caregiver's agenda and adopts it as his or her own.

APPLICATION

Situation

Mrs. Smith is shopping with her 2-year-old daughter, Sarah. Sarah keeps taking things off the shelf and putting them in the shopping cart. Mrs. Smith is starting to get upset. Compare this situation to what you read in the sections on the "Forbidden Toy Technique" and on self-control.

Questions to answer

1. What strategies would you advise Mrs. Smith to use to keep Sarah from taking things off the shelf?

2. What strategies that she might already be using would likely backfire with a 2-year-old? Why?

3. Would your advice be different if Sarah were 6- or 7-years old?

USING WHAT YOU HAVE LEARNED

Following graduation, you get a job working as a psychological consultant with the local school. The school is concerned that there seem to be some children who aren't able to deal well with negative feedback concerning their school performance. Often when they encounter failure, they don't believe they "have what it takes" to do well at school. The school principal asks you to help answer the following questions:

1. Do children really react differently to the same experiences, so that some cope well with failure and keep trying, while others give up?

2. What factors might cause such differences between types of children?

3. Could it have to do with how children are treated in the classroom? Is there anything teachers could do to help the children who don't cope well?

4. Is this really important anyway? Will children just grow out of this, or should we be concerned?

Based on what you've read in Chapter 13 concerning academic self-concept, especially Dweck's motivational model of achievement, how would you address these questions?

SAMPLE TEST QUESTIONS

1. Children's opinions of themselves and their abilities are referred to as:

    a. self-knowledge
    b. self-evaluation
    c. self-centeredness
    d. egocentrism

2. The part of the self-system that would be concerned with children's ability to resist temptation is:

    a. self-knowledge
    b. self evaluation
    c. self-regulation
    d. self-centeredness

3. The notion of self-schemas is attributable to which approach?

    a. Piaget's theory
    b. Selman's model
    c. Information-Processing model
    d. Self-Efficacy theory

4. According to Selman's research, believing that the self cannot ever be completely known characterizes which period of development?

    a. early childhood
    b. middle childhood
    c. preadolescence
    d. adolescence

5. The belief that inner thoughts and feelings are directly represented in outward appearance or behavior characterizes which level of Selman's model of children's awareness of the self?

    a. level 0
    b. level 1
    c. level 2
    d. level 3

6. Children who are high in self-esteem and who are not depressed are more likely to recall:

    a. negative personal traits
    b. positive personal traits
    c. about equal proportions of positive and negative personal traits
    d. it would be impossible to predict how they would recall the traits

7.   The notion of self-efficacy is associated with which theorist?

    a.   Bandura   b.   Dweck
    c.   Harter   d.   Selman

8.   In contrast to European American children, Japanese children

    a.   are taught to sacrifice their personal interest for the sake of interpersonal harmony
    b.   are taught to defend their individual rights and to respect the rights of others
    c.   are taught that they have the right to an opinion very early in life
    d.   are socialized for independence from an early age

9.   In one study, babies aged 6 months and older watched an adult model eat a Cheerio. They were then given one instructed either to feed it to themselves or feed it to their mothers. Results indicated that

    a.   more infants fed the Cheerio to their mothers than to themselves
    b.   infants were equally inclined to feed the Cheerio to themselves or to their mothers
    c.   most infants simply played with the Cheerio rather than feeding themselves or their mothers
    d.   more infants fed the Cheerio to themselves than to their mothers

10.   An infant looking in a mirror notices a red mark on her forehead in the reflection and touches her forehead. This behavior does not occur until at least _____ of age.

    a.   8 months
    b.   12 months
    c.   15 months
    d.   24 months

11.   Synchronic imitation in the play of preverbal children shows evidence of:

    a.   other awareness
    b.   self-knowledge
    c.   self-recognition
    d.   self- and other-regulation

12.   When asked to describe himself, Daniel replies: "I love guitar, and I'm really an easy-going kind of guy." Based on research into children's self-descriptions, we may conclude that Daniel is likely:

    a.   3-years old
    b.   5-years old
    c.   8-years old
    d.   13-years old

13.   When asked what kind of person she is, Francine replies: "I have very long hair and I live in a white house." Francine's self-description indicates that she is likely at what Piagetian stage of development?

    a.   sensorimotor
    b.   preoperational
    c.   concrete operational
    d.   formal operational

14.   Eleven-year old Suzie has begun to question her abilities, her appearance, and so on, although she used to be a fairly optimistic, confident little girl. Her parents have noticed the change, and are concerned. What would you tell them?

    a.   This is a serious change, and likely signals even further problems to come as she enters high school.
    b.   This is a serious problem, and likely has been with her since kindergarten; her parents were likely mistaken when they assumed she had been self-confident earlier on.
    c.   Her parents are likely wrong; it is very unlikely for self-esteem to be an issue before adolescence.
    d.   This is a fairly common occurrence; it may not be a major cause for concern since many children's esteem increases again during the high school years.

15.   Which of the following is LEAST likely to be related to decreasing self-esteem as children approach adolescence?

    a.   remaining in the same school
    b.   biological changes associated with puberty
    c.   increasing self-consciousness
    d.   ALL of the above are EQUALLY associated with drops in self-esteem

16.   According to Dweck's model, children who display the helpless pattern generally believe that:

    a.   their lack of success is the result of a lack of ability
    b.   effort is more important to success than ability
    c.   their lack of success comes from lack of ability, but that ability can grow through experience
    d.   all of the above

17.   In terms of the emergence of self-control, most children begin to pay attention to simple standards set by others or by themselves, and monitor their activities with respect to those standards during the _____ year of age.

    a.   first   b.   second
    c.   third   d.   fourth

18.   Which of the following is likely to influence children's behavior in the forbidden-toy procedure?

a.   Teaching children to develop their own plans or strategies for dealing with the temptation to play with the toy.
b.   Providing children with a good rationale for the prohibition against playing with the toy.
c.   Seeing an adult break the rule and play with the toy.
d.   All of the above

19.   Which of the following is true concerning delay of gratification?

a.   Ability to delay of gratification is not a very stable characteristic, fluctuating wildly from childhood to adolescence.
b.   Ability to delay gratification seems related to children's social competence.
c.   Preschoolers display an impressive understanding of delay-of-gratification strategies, even at such a young age.
d.   all of the above

20.   The ability to delay gratification in the preschool years is predictive of children's functioning 10 years later in which of the following areas?

a.   self-knowledge
b.   creativity
c.   coping with stress
d.   artistic appreciation

ANSWERS

FILL-IN EXERCISES

1. existential, categorical   2. knowledge (awareness); evaluation; regulation 3. awareness (or knowledge)
4. schemas   5. efficacy 6. self-reactions 7. personal agency 8. synchronic imitation   9. me, mine
10. fifteen; twenty-four   11. two 12. false-self 13. looking-glass 14. esteem   15. kindergarten
16. mastery; helpless 17. entity; incremental 18. lower 19. fathers   20. possible selves 21. committed

SAMPLE TEST QUESTIONS

1. b	11. a
2. c	12. d
3. c	13. b
4. d	14. d
5. b	15. a
6. b	16. a
7. a	17. c
8. a	18. d
9. d	19. b
10. c	20. c

Chapter 14
Moral Development

OUTLINE

Use this outline as you read the chapter. Enter your questions, comments, and notes in the space provided. Write down terms or statements you don't understand, with their page numbers.

THEORIES OF MORAL DEVELOPMENT

Cognitive-Developmental Approaches

Evolutionary and Biological Approaches

Environmental/Learning Approaches

Sociocultural Approaches

MORAL REASONING

Evaluating Piaget's Model

Evaluating Kohlberg's Model

Evaluating Turiel's Model

Distributive Justice and Retributive Justice

Social and Family Influences on Moral Reasoning

On the Cutting Edge
Children's Reasoning about the Morality of Peer Exclusion

Moral Reasoning and Moral Conduct

Classics of Research
A Study in Moral Character: Are There "Good Kids" and "Bad Kids"?

PROSOCIAL BEHAVIOR

Empathy and Sympathy

Development of Prosocial Behavior

Biological Determinants of Prosocial Behavior

Cognitive and Affective Determinants of Prosocial Behavior

Sociocultural and Family Determinants of Prosocial Behavior

AGGRESSION

Defining Aggression

Age and Gender Differences in Aggression

Biological Determinants of Aggression

Sociocultural and Environmental Determinants of Aggression

Cognitive and Affective Influences on Aggression

Controlling Aggression

Applications
Bullying and Victimization in School

LEARNING OBJECTIVES

Upon completion of Chapter 14 you should be able to discuss the following topics. Check off those you are confident that you can discuss well. Re-read the material in the text for the topics about which you are less confident. Record the important points from your reading in the space below each topic.

1.   Outline and describe Piaget's four stages of moral reasoning.

2.   Explain how interactions with peers influence moral development, according to Piaget's theory.

3.   Describe Kohlberg's cognitive theory of moral development, outlining the three levels of moral reasoning, and the two stages comprising each level.

4.   Discuss how Turiel's model explains moral reasoning.

5.   Present the evolutionary/biological position regarding altruistic and aggressive behavior.

6.   Explain how social learning theory views moral development.

7.   Discuss how sociocultural approaches view moral development.

8.   Describe how research has supported Piaget's theory of moral development. What aspects of the theory have not held up well to empirical scrutiny?

9. Discuss the aspects of Kohlberg's theory that have been supported and that have not been supported by empirical research.

10. Discuss the findings of research evaluating the claims of Turiel's model of moral reasoning.

11. Explain how children reason concerning both distributive and retributive justice.

12. Briefly describe how peer and parents influence moral reasoning.

13. Distinguish between each of the following classes of parental discipline: power assertion, love withdrawal, and induction. How are these classes of discipline related to moral internalization?

14. Briefly explain how Piaget, Kohlberg, and social-learning theorists view the relationship between moral reasoning and moral conduct.

15. Outline Hoffman's five stages in the development of empathy.

16. Discuss the findings of research examining helping and sharing in young children.

17. Distinguish between the following three methods of conflict resolution in children: negotiation, disengagement, and coercion. How does the use of these strategies change with age?

18.   Discuss how age and culture may be important considerations in children's peacemaking.

19.   Explain how genetic factors might produce differences in prosocial behavior.

20.   Briefly discuss how empathy, prosocial reasoning, and mental state understanding contribute to children's prosocial behavior.

21.   Describe how parents can influence children's prosocial behavior through each of the following ways: providing opportunities for prosocial behavior, communicating values to children, and by modeling and reinforcing prosocial behavior.

22.   Differentiate verbal aggression from physical aggression.

23.   Distinguish between hostile aggression, instrumental aggression, and relational aggression.

24.   Explain how each of the following three mechanisms may indicate a biological basis for aggression:

hormones

genes

temperament

25.   Describe how the expression of aggression changes across age, and how aggression displayed by boys differs from that displayed by girls.

26. Describe how family process, such as modeling and coercive interactions, may encourage aggressive behavior in children.

27. Argue against the notion that all aggressive children have no friends.

28. Discuss what researchers have found concerning children's exposure to violence on television and in real life.

29. Discuss the social-cognitive differences that have been found between aggressive and non-aggressive children.

30. Describe several successful techniques for reducing aggression in children.

KEY TERMS

Upon completion of Chapter 14, you should be able to define the following terms.

Moral dilemmas _____

_____

Moral realism _____

_____

Immanent justice _____

_____

Moral relativism _____

_____

Preconventional level   _____

_____

Conventional level   _____

_____

Postconventional level   _____

_____

Social conventions   _____

_____

Paradox of altruism   _____

_____

Kin selection   _____

_____

Reciprocal altruism   _____

_____

Dominance hierarchy   _____

_____

Prosocial behavior   _____

_____

Empathy   _____

_____

Sympathy _____

_____

Peacemaking _____

_____

Aggression _____

_____

Hostile (retaliatory) aggression _____

_____

Instrumental aggression _____

_____

Relational aggression _____

_____

Coercive family process _____

_____

Displaced aggression _____

_____

Catharsis _____

_____

FILL-IN EXERCISES

Fill in the word or words that best fit in the spaces below.

1.   Investigations that focus on children's behavior in moral situations examine moral _____, whereas those looking at how children think about their behavior examine moral _____.

2.   Piaget examined children playing games such as marbles because of his interest in how they created and enforced _____.

3.   Young children's notion that punishment must always occur when a rule is broken was described by Piaget as _____ _____.

4.   Considering motives and intentions to be as important as the outcomes of behavior characterizes Piaget's stage of _____ _____.

5.   From his research, Kohlberg concluded that moral reasoning develops in three predictable levels, which he termed _____, _____, and _____, each of which contains _____ stages.

6.   Kohlberg's model shares several characteristics with that of Piaget. Each stage forms a structured _____, with children in that stage generally responding consistently to different dilemmas and situations. The stages follow a(n) _____ sequence, so that children experience them all in the same order, with no regression to previous stages. Finally, the pattern of progression is _____ for all people and all cultures.

7.   Turiel believes that children's moral reasoning involves three distinct domains. The _____ domain is concerned with people's rights and welfare. The _____ domain involves social conventions. Finally, there are matters of personal choice, in which individual preferences take priority.

8.   Behaviors that benefit someone else, but offer no obvious benefit to the individual performing them, are _____ behaviors.

9.   The notion of _____ selection proposes that humans behave in ways that increase the chances for the survival and reproduction of their genes rather than of themselves.

10.   _____ altruism is a process that suggests that people are programmed to be helpful because (1) it increases the likelihood that some day they will in turn receive aid from the person they helped, or (2) that by helping someone else in their social group they ensure the survival of genes similar to their own.

11.   A _____ _____ refers to a structured social group in which members higher on the power ladder control those who are lower, through aggression and threats.

12. Cross-cultural studies of Kohlberg's theory find that in many nontechnical countries, individuals rarely progress to the _____ stage.

13. The issue of how to distribute a limited amount of resources among a group of deserving people is referred to as _____ _____.

14. Use of commands, threats, and physical force is a disciplinary practice referred to as _____ _____; the use of verbal disapproval, ridicule, or withholding of affection is described as _____ _____.

15. The disciplinary practice that is associated with the most advanced levels of moral reasoning in American children is _____.

16. _____ refers to the ability to vicariously experience another's emotional state or condition, whereas _____ involves feeling concern for another in reaction to his or her situation or emotional state, without necessarily sharing the same emotions.

17. Babies crying when they hear another baby crying may be an early sign of _____.

18. Conflict can be resolved in three broad ways. _____ includes compromise and intervention by a third party, such as another peer or a teacher. _____ includes withdrawal and shifting the focus or topic. _____ occurs when one party gives in to the demands of another, sometimes in response to threats or other aggressive ploys.

19. A friendly postconflict reunion between former opponents is described as _____.

20. Name-calling, teasing, and threats are referred to as _____ aggression, whereas hitting, kicking, and biting are called _____ aggression.

21. Aggression aimed at inflicting pain or injury is called _____ aggression, whereas aggressive behavior whose purpose is to obtain something is termed _____ aggression.

22. Beginning in the preschool years and extending into adolescence, girls are more likely to display _____ aggression than are boys.

23. There is evidence that the hormone _____ plays a role in aggression.

24. Gerald Patterson referred to the method by which some families control one another through aggression and other coercive means as _____ _____ _____.

25. Retaliatory aggression directed at a person or object other than the one against whom retaliation is desired is referred to as _____ _____.

26.   _____ is a psychoanalytic belief that the likelihood of aggression can be reduced by viewing aggression or by engaging in high-energy behaviors. This belief _____ (*has/has not*) been supported by research.

USING WHAT YOU HAVE LEARNED

Children are participating in an interview designed to assess their moral reasoning, using a variation of Piaget's moral dilemmas. The interviewer presents the following situations:

Jeffrey is called to dinner by his mother. While coming to dinner he accidentally knocks over a tray of dishes that was behind the door to the dining room, breaking 10 cups.

James has been told not to take any cookies from the cupboard. He goes ahead anyway, and while taking a cookie, breaks a saucer.

The interviewer asks each subject whether Jeffrey or James did the worse thing, and what punishment each deserves. What do the following responses indicate about the children's moral reasoning?

#1 by Robert. "James deserves more punishment, but Jeffrey doesn't. Jeffrey didn't really mean it."

#2 by Maria. "Both deserve equal punishment. They broke nice things that don't belong to them."

#3 by Tim. "Jeffrey did the worse thing because he broke more things."

APPLICATION

You have been asked to write a short pamphlet offering advice for parents concerning how to promote the development of prosocial behavior and discourage aggressive behavior in their children. The pamphlet is intended to touch on the following topics:

1. When and how to reward and punish your child.

2. Should you be concerned about the effects of television?

3. Talking to your child about moral issues.

4. Teaching your child how to deal with conflict.

5. Differences between boys and girls.

Based on what you have read in Chapter 14, what advice would you give to parents with reference to each of these five topics?

SAMPLE TEST QUESTIONS

1.   Piaget investigated children's understanding of rules by:

   a.   observing them playing marbles
   b.   presenting them with prosocial dilemmas in which the individual must decide whether to help someone, often at some personal expense
   c.   presenting them with moral dilemmas that involve choosing between obeying a rule or breaking a rule for the benefit of an individual
   d.   presenting them with rewards and asking them to divide them up equitably among their peers

2.   All of the following are characteristic of Piaget's second stage of moral development, except:

   a.   consideration of amount of damage when judging whether an act is morally wrong
   b.   consideration of an individual's intentions when judging whether an act is morally wrong
   c.   view of rules as absolute
   d.   belief that punishment must always occur if a rule is broken

3.   Piaget uses the term heteronomous to refer to:

    a.   the notion that punishment must always occur if a rule is broken
    b.   the tendency to evaluate moral situations only in terms of their objective and physical consequences
    c.   the belief that punishment must always occur if a rule is broken
    d.   the belief that morality is dictated by people in authority

4.   Children in Piaget's third stage of moral development view rules as:

    a.   unchangeable absolutes
    b.   agreements that can be changed to fit the circumstances of the moment
    c.   dictated by people in authority
    d.   applicable only to their peers (i.e., their age-mates)

5.   While driving with his father, little Billy notices a speed-limit sign. He asks his father what the sign means and his father explains that it means they shouldn't drive faster than 55 miles per hour. Billy then asks his father how fast they're driving and becomes really upset to find they're driving 60 miles per hour. According to Piaget's theory of moral development, Billy is likely how old?

    a.   three years   b.   five years
    c.   nine years   d.   eleven years

6.   Movement from stage to stage in Kohlberg's model closely follows the Piagetian process of:

    a.   assimilation
    b.   seriation
    c.   accommodation
    d.   reversibility

7.   Someone at Kohlberg's preconventional level evaluates moral dilemmas according to:

    a.   his/her own self-interests and needs
    b.   the principles of fairness and justice
    c.   the concern for maintaining social order
    d.   the concern for social approval

8.   Social learning theorists argue that:

    a.   moral development parallels stages of cognitive development
    b.   observational learning, reinforcement, and punishment account for children's moral development
    c.   children progress through a sequence of stages of moral development that is universal
    d.   there is a strong connection between moral reasoning and moral conduct

9. Which of the following claims of Turiel's model has been supported by recent research?

   a. moral reasoning involves several independent domains of social cognition
   b. induction fosters moral development to a greater extent than either love withdrawal or power assertion
   c. young children do not consider intent when making moral judgments
   d. all children must progress through the same stages of moral development, in the same order

10. Until about _____ years of age, children's distribution of rewards to others is characterized by self-interest.

    a. two
    b. four
    c. six
    d. eight

11. By seven years of age, children use _____ as the basis for distributing rewards to others.

    a. equity
    b. equality
    c. altruism
    d. empathy

12. The form of discipline that produces the least mature forms of moral reasoning is:

    a. induction
    b. love withdrawal
    c. power assertion
    d. love assertion

13. Martin Hoffman has proposed a 5-stage model of the development of empathy. During the fourth stage:

    a. Because they now can understand that others have inner states different than their own, children offer appropriate help and comfort.
    b. Children have difficulty distinguishing between their own and others' thoughts and feelings, and so offer help that reflects what they would like, rather than what the other person needs.
    c. Children respond to the distress of others by comforting themselves or by seeking comfort from caregivers.
    d. Children reflexively cry when they hear another child crying.

14. Aggressive behavior whose purpose is to obtain something is referred to as:

    a. hostile aggression
    b. displaced aggression
    c. verbal aggression
    d. instrumental aggression

15.   Which of the following is **NOT** true concerning gender differences in aggression?

  a.   boys display more aggression in preschool than do girls
  b.   in elementary school, boys become increasingly aggressive towards girls
  c.   beginning in preschool and extending into adolescence, girls display more relational aggression than do boys
  d.   in elementary school, aggression by boys toward other boys becomes increasingly physical in nature

16.   Studies examining the effects of televised violence report that:

  a.   children imitate violent acts seen on television
  b.   TV violence increases the likelihood of all others forms of aggression in children, even those that do not resemble the behavior of the television models
  c.   television violence stimulates aggression, and children who are more aggressive tend to watch even more violent television
  d.   all of the above

17.   Cairn's research concerning the friendship patterns of aggressive children found:

  a.   aggressive children had much fewer peer nominations of "best friend" than did nonaggressive children
  b.   aggressive children were most often nominated as "best friend" by non-aggressive peers rather than other aggressive children
  c.   aggressive children tended to be largely shunned by the peer group, resulting in no peer nominations at all
  d.   aggressive children had just as many peer nominations of "best friend" as did non-aggressive children

18.   Coercive family process involves:

  a.   family members controlling one another through aggression and other coercive means
  b.   coercing a family to deal with an aggressive child through the process of family therapy
  c.   family members controlling one another through coercive means such as bribery and monetary rewards
  d.   a means by which some families attempt to coerce an aggressive child to be non-aggressive through the use of rewards alone

19.   In comparison to non-aggressive children, aggressive children:

  a.   show a lower level of moral reasoning
  b.   show less empathy
  c.   are more likely to attribute hostile motives to other children
  d.   all of the above

20.   Which of the following has **NOT** proven effective in controlling aggression?

    a.   catharsis
    b.   parent training
    c.   social-cognitive methods
    d.   all of the above **HAVE** been found effective

ANSWERS

FILL-IN EXERCISES

1. conduct; reasoning   2. rules   3. immanent justice   4. moral relativism   5. preconventional, conventional, postconventional; two 6. whole; invariant, universal 7. moral; social   8. altruistic   9. kin 10. reciprocal   11. dominance hierarchy   12. fifth   13. distributive justice   14. power assertion; love withdrawal 15. induction   16. empathy; sympathy 17. empathy   18. negotiation; disengagement; coercion 19. peacemaking 20. verbal, physical   21. hostile (or retaliatory); instrumental 22. relational 23. testosterone 24. coercive family process 25.displaced aggression   26. catharsis; has not

SAMPLE TEST QUESTIONS

1. a	11. a
2. b	12. c
3. d	13. a
4. b	14. d
5. b	15. b
6. c	16. d
7. a	17. d
8. b	18. a
9. a	19. d
10. b	20. a

Chapter 15
Gender-Role Development and Sex Differences

OUTLINE

Use this outline as you read the chapter. Enter your questions, comments, and notes in the space provided. Write down terms or statements you don't understand, with their page numbers.

THEORIES OF GENDER-ROLE DEVELOPMENT AND SEX DIFFERENCES

Evolutionary and Biological Approaches

Sociocultural Approaches

Cognitive-Developmental Approaches

Environmental/Learning Approaches

SOME PERCEIVED AND REAL SEX DIFFERENCES

Physical Differences

Cognitive Differences

Applications
Should Schools Teach Visual Spatial Skills?

Social and Personality Differences

BIOLOGICAL INFLUENCES ON GENDER-ROLE DEVELOPMENT

Genetic Influences

Hormonal Influences

Brain Lateralization

Classics of Research
Prenatal Influences on Gender Identity: The Case of David Reimer

SOCIALIZATION AND GENDER-ROLE DEVELOPMENT

Socialization by Society

Socialization by Parents

Socialization by Peers

On The Cutting Edge
The Influence of Opposite-Sex Siblings on Interests, Activities, and Behavior

Socialization by Self

UNDERSTANDING GENDER ROLES AND STEREOTYPES

The Development of Gender Identity

The Development of Gender Knowledge

Flexibility of Gender Knowledge

Gender Knowledge and Behavior

DEVELOPMENT OF SEXUAL RELATIONSHIPS AND BEHAVIOR

Emergence of Romantic and Sexual Interest

Origins of Sexual Orientation

LEARNING OBJECTIVES

Upon completion of Chapter 15 you should be able to discuss the following topics. Check off those you are confident that you can discuss well. Re-read the material in the text for the topics about which you are less confident. Record the important points from your reading in the space below each topic.

1.   Describe the evolutionary and psychobiological approaches to sex differences and explain how these approaches differ from sociocultural approaches.

2.   Outline the three stages that, according to Kohlberg, represent the child's understanding of gender constancy.

3.   Explain the origins and effects of gender schemas.

4.   Compare and contrast gender schema theory with Kohlberg's gender constancy theory.

5.   Explain how social learning theorists account for gender-role development.

6.   Describe the physical differences between males and females, focusing on differences in physical maturity and vulnerability, activity level, and motor development.

7.   Explain how males and females differ in terms of language and verbal abilities.

8.   Discuss the differences found between boys and girls in mathematical abilities, and explain how strategy preferences may contribute to such differences.

9.   Describe the differences in spatial abilities found between boys and girls, and discuss two possible explanations for such differences.

10.   Describe the aspects of infant temperament found to differ between boys and girls.

11.   Explain the differences between girls and boys in emotional development.

12.   Describe how girls differ from boys in the development of self-control.

13.   Discuss how boys and girls differ in aggression and prosocial behavior.

14.   Explain how girls and boys differ in activities and interests.

15.   Describe the differences found between girls' and boys' peer relationships.

16.   Explain how genetic and hormonal factors contribute to sex differentiation.

17.   Describe the following two hormonal abnormalities: *congenital adrenal hyperplasia (CAH)* and *androgen insensitivity.*

18.   Discuss the relevance of the case of David Reimer to the issue of the roles of biology and socialization in determining gender identity.

19.   Describe how differences between males and females in brain lateralization may play a role in gender differences.

20.   Explain the roles played by society (i.e., modeling and differential treatment of males and females) in the socialization of gender roles. What has research shown about the role teachers may play?

22.   Explain the roles played by parents (i.e., modeling and differential treatment of males and females) in the socialization of gender roles, commenting on differences in how mothers and fathers socialize their sons and daughters.

23.   Discuss the roles of peers and siblings in the socialization of gender roles.

24. Explain how children participate in their own socialization of gender roles.

25. Describe how children's gender knowledge and the flexibility of their gender stereotypes develop across age.

26. Explain how children's gender knowledge affects their behavior in the areas of toy preferences, motivation, memory, and social judgments.

27. Describe the development of romantic and sexual interest in children.

28. Discuss how biology and socialization may influence sexual orientation, and describe the interactionist model proposed by Darryl Bem.

KEY TERMS

Upon completion of Chapter 15, you should be able to define the following terms.

Sex differentiation _____

_____

Gender role _____

_____

Sex typing _____

_____

Gender constancy   _____

_____

Gender identity _____

_____

Gender stability _____

_____

Gender consistency   _____

_____

Gender schemas   _____

_____

Lateralization   _____

_____

Sex-limited traits   _____

_____

Congenital adrenal hyperplasia (CAH)   _____

_____

Androgen insensitivity   _____

_____

FILL-IN EXERCISES

Fill in the word or words that best fit in the spaces below.

1.   The term _____ _____ refers to a pattern or set of behaviors considered appropriate for males and females within a particular culture.

2.   According to evolutionary approaches, _____ *(males/females)* tend to be choosier about their mates and invest more in parenting.

3. According to the _____ approach, gender roles develop as children participate in and prepare for the adult roles they are expected to play in their communities.

4. Kohlberg proposed that gender constancy develops in three stages – gender _____, gender _____, and gender _____.

5. _____ _____ are cognitive representations of the characteristics associated with being either male or female.

6. At birth, the _____ (*male/female*) newborn is generally healthier and more developmentally advanced.

7. On average, _____ (*boys/girls*) have higher activity levels, a difference that extends through infancy and childhood.

8. _____ (*boys/girls*) show an advantage in gross motor skills that require a combination of balance and precise movement.

9. Throughout the school years _____ (*boys/girls*) achieve higher scores in reading and writing.

10. Brain _____ refers to the specialization of functions in the right and left hemispheres of the brain.

11. First-grade girls are more likely to use _____ mathematical strategies, whereas boys are more likely to use _____ approaches.

12. There is some evidence that sex differences in spatial abilities _____ (*increase/decrease*) in adolescence and adulthood.

13. _____ (*male/female*) infants seem better equipped for socialization. They maintain greater eye contact, engage in more face-to-face communication, and smile more.

14. Sex differences have been reported in strategies used to regulate emotional states. Toddlers were promised an attractive toy but made to wait before being allowed to play with it. The _____ (*boys/girls*) coped with the stress of the situation by seeking comfort from their mothers, whereas the _____ (*boys/girls*) were more likely to distract themselves by playing with other objects in the room.

15. Boys are _____ (*more/less*) likely to express anger, _____ (*more/less*) likely to deny feeling afraid, and _____ (*more/less*) likely to follow cultural display rules regarding the expression of disappointment.

16. Prior to age _____, girls and boys engage in disruptive and impulsive behavior equally often. After this age, however, _____ (*boys/girls*) show a steady decline in behavior problems, whereas _____ (*boys/girls*) show a lesser decline and, in some cases, even an increase.

17.   In elementary school, girls show _____ interest in mathematics and science compared to boys.

18.   Specific interests within the domain of science differ between boys and girls. Male students tend to express more interest in the _____ sciences, whereas female students express more interest in the _____ sciences.

19.   Beginning in early childhood, _____ (*boys/girls*) play in larger groups, whereas _____ (*boys/girls*) generally limit their group size to two or three.

20.   Like most other species, humans exhibit sexual _____ -- that is, the male and female are biologically different for the purpose of reproduction. The process through which these biological differences emerge is called sex _____.

21.   Traits resulting from genes that affect males and females differently, but that are not carried on the sex chromosomes, are referred to as _____-_____ traits.

22.   When a Y chromosome causes testes to develop in the embryo, these glands secrete hormones called _____, which cause the male internal organs to grow.

23.   _____ _____ _____ is a recessive genetic disorder in which the adrenal glands produce unusually high levels of male hormones, regardless of the presence or absence of testes.

24.   Studies show consistently that teachers give more attention to _____ (*boys/girls*) than to _____ (*boys/girls*).

25.   During infancy, parents are more likely to physically stimulate _____ (*boys/girls*) than _____ (*boys/girls*).

26.   Parents' gender typing of play tends to be stronger with _____ (*sons/daughters*) than with _____ (*sons/daughters*). This is especially true of _____ (*mothers/fathers*).

27.   Data from a number of studies have confirmed Kohlberg's stage model of gender constancy. By 3 years of age, almost all children display gender _____. Gender _____ follows at about 4 years of age, and gender _____ at about 5.

28.   Gender knowledge has been found to influence children's memory. Children's recall is better when it is _____ with the gender schemas they have formed.

29.   By middle adolescence, approximately _____ of U.S. adolescents are involved in a romantic relationship.

30.   Surveys in North America and Europe estimated the percentage of men who identify themselves as gay to be around _____ to _____ of the population and the percentage of women who identify themselves as lesbian to be around _____ to _____.

31.   Bem has proposed a model – termed the _____-_____-_____ theory -- of how biological factors and experience might interact in the development of sexual orientation.

APPLICATION

You have read in Chapter 15 about differences between boys and girls in certain cognitive abilities and certain social and personality characteristics. Some of these may have a biological basis; some may be the result of differences in how adults socialize children; most of them probably involve an interaction between nature and nurture. Using what you have read in Chapter 15, consider how nature and nurture may play a role in the following sex differences, and especially consider how they may interact.

1.   On the average, girls have greater abilities in many types of verbal skills than boys.

2.   By adolescence males express greater interest in mathematics than do females. They also begin to perform significantly better than females, at least when measured on standardized exams.

3.   On the average, boys seem to be better at spatial tasks, such as mental-rotation tasks, a sex difference that may increase during adolescence.

4.   On the average, boys have higher activity levels than girls. Interestingly, sex differences in activity level are small when children are playing alone; however, boys' activity levels increase substantially when they are in the company of other boys.

5.   Boys generally display more aggressive behavior than girls.

USING WHAT YOU HAVE LEARNED

What are Some Common Beliefs About Sex Differences?

Many people hold stereotypical beliefs about sex differences. It can be interesting to compare these with what research actually shows about how males and females differ. To get an idea of some of these beliefs, ask several of your friends how boys and girls differ and what they think is the source of these differences.

1.   What seem to be the most common beliefs?

2.   Is there an age difference in beliefs? That is, do older people have different beliefs than younger people?

3.   Is there a gender difference in beliefs? That is, do males hold different beliefs, or offer different explanations for the source of gender differences, than females?

4.   Does providing objective information about gender differences alter people's beliefs? Think about your own beliefs before and after reading Chapter 15. Did they change?

SAMPLE TEST QUESTIONS

1. The process by which biological sex differences emerge is referred to as:

    a. sex typing
    b. gender typing
    c. gender identity formation
    d. sex differentiation

2. According to Kohlberg's theory, children pass through three stages in the development of gender constancy. The order of these stages is:

    a. gender identity, gender stability, gender consistency
    b. gender consistency, gender identity, gender stability
    c. gender identity, gender consistency, gender stability
    d. gender stability, gender identity, gender consistency

3. Sociocultural theorists contend that

    a. sex differences observed among children and adults follow from the roles commonly held by females versus males
    b. inborn, intrinsic differences between the sexes give rise to and maintain gender roles
    c. the cognitive representations children have of the characteristics associated with being either male or female underlie children's gender-role behavior
    d. sex-typed behaviors are the product of reinforcement and modeling

4. All of the following are ways in which female newborns differ from male newborns, **EXCEPT:**

    a. the female is healthier and more developmentally advanced than the male
    b. the female is less muscular than the male
    c. the female is less sensitive to pain than the male
    d. the female is better coordinated neurologically and physically

5. By about age 5, boys perform better than girls on tasks requiring

    a. balance and precise movement
    b. fine motor skills
    c. strength
    d. all of the above

6. Which of the following is untrue concerning language and verbal abilities in female infants?

    a. Female infants produce fewer sounds than do males.
    b. Female infants use words earlier than males
    c. Female infants have a larger vocabulary than males.
    d. All of the above **ARE** true.

7.   Which of the following is true concerning the mathematical strategies preferred by girls?

    a.   Girls prefer to use logic, estimation, and unconventional strategies to solve mathematical problems.

    b.   Girls prefer the conventional strategies that are taught in school.

    c.   Starting in the first grade, girls prefer to use more sophisticated strategies than do boys.

    d.   All of the above

8.   Ross Vasta and colleagues' finding that bartenders and servers perform better than adults of equal age, gender, and education on the water-level task suggests that

    a.   performance on the water-level task is culturally specific

    b.   practical experience can enhance spatial competence

    c.   spatial competence is largely biologically based

    d.   spatial competence is evolutionarily based

9.   Which of the following is untrue concerning the social interactions of female infants?

    a.   Female infants maintain greater eye contact with their caregivers than males.

    b.   Female infants engage in more face-to-face communication than males.

    c.   Female infants smile more during social interactions than do males.

    d.   Female infants are more sociable than males.

10.   In terms of the development of self-control,

    a.   boys develop self-regulatory capabilities more rapidly than girls

    b.   boys comply more readily and at a younger age than girls

    c.   boys engage in more disruptive and impulsive behavior than girls, even as toddlers

    d.   none of the above

11.   Which of the following is untrue concerning aggression and prosocial behavior in girls and boys?

    a.   Boys display more physical aggression than girls.

    b.   Girls are more likely to display relational and social forms of aggression than boys.

    c.   Girls tend to display more prosocial behavior than boys.

    d.   Actually, all of the above **ARE** true.

12.   The sex chromosomes

    a.   influence the prenatal development of the male gonads at about 6 weeks

    b.   influence the prenatal development of the female gonads at about 6 weeks

    c.   play a crucial role in sex differentiation throughout the prenatal period

    d.   all of the above

13.   Congenital adrenal hyperplasia results in:

    a.   higher levels of aggressive and antisocial behavior in boys
    b.   masculinized interests and activities in girls
    c.   feminized interests and activities in boys
    d.   markedly high spatial abilities in boys

14.   How do teachers often react when children engage in cross-sex activities?

    a.   Both boys and girls receive criticism equally for engaging in cross-sex activities.
    b.   Both boys and girls are encouraged to engage in cross-sex activities.
    c.   Girls receive criticism for engaging in cross-sex activities more than boys.
    d.   Boys receive criticism for engaging in cross-sex activities more than girls.

15.   How do fathers differ from mothers in the role they play in gender-role development?

    a.   Mothers play the largest role; fathers, because they spend less time with their children, contribute very little.
    b.   Mothers are concerned that their daughters be feminine, fathers are concerned that their sons be masculine.
    c.   Fathers are concerned that their daughters be feminine and their sons be masculine, whereas mothers are less concerned about the gender-appropriateness of their children's behavior.
    d.   Mothers are concerned that their daughters be feminine and their sons be masculine, whereas fathers are less concerned about the gender-appropriateness of their children's behavior.

16.   When do parents begin to view boys and girls differently?

    a.   at birth
    b.   shortly after the first birthday
    c.   during the toddler period
    d.   during the preschool period

17.   Children can reliably sort pictures of males and females and their "accessories" such as toys, tools, and appliances by about what age?

    a.   one year
    b.   two years
    c.   three years
    d.   four years

18.   When shown a series of photographs, each depicting either a male or a female performing a sex-stereotyped activity (e.g., a woman or a man ironing clothes), when asked which pictures they had seen earlier, children:

   a.   more accurately remembered gender-inconsistent information than consistent information, probably because it seemed so different to them that it stuck in their minds
   c.   remembered both gender consistent and inconsistent information equally well
   d.   could not remember either gender consistent or inconsistent information, since visual memory is so poor in children
   d.   more accurately remembered gender-consistent than inconsistent information

19.   Boys and girls typically report experiencing their first romantic interests, or "crushes"

   a.   between the ages of 5 and 7
   b.   between the ages of 7 and 10
   c.   between the ages of 10 and 14
   d.   between the ages of 15 and 16

20.   Which of the following is true concerning homosexual boys?

   a.   Homosexual boys tend frequently to be first-borns.
   b.   Homosexual boys tend to be the only boy in a family with many older sisters.
   c.   Homosexual boys are m ore likely to have several older brothers than heterosexual boys.
   d.   Homosexual boys tend frequently to have a father who is gay.

ANSWERS

FILL-IN EXERCISES

1. gender role   2. females   3. sociocultural   4. identity, stability, consistency   5. gender schemas
6. female   7. boys   8. girls   9 girls   10. lateralization   11. concrete; abstract
12. increase   13. female   14. girls; boys   15. more; more; less   16. 4 or 5 years; girls; boys
17 equal   18. physical; biological   19. boys; girls   20. dimorphism; differentiation   21. sex-limited
22. androgens   23. congenital adrenal hyperplasia (CAH)   24. boys; girls   25. boys; girls
26. sons; daughters; fathers   27. identity; stability, four; consistency   28. consistent   29. half
30. 3%, 5%; 2%, 3%   31. Exotic-Becomes-Erotic

SAMPLE TEST QUESTIONS

1. d	11. c
2. a	12. a
3. a	13. b
4. c	14. d
5. c	15. c
6. a	16. a
7. b	17. b
8. b	18. d
9. d	19. b
10. d	20. c

Chapter 16
Families and Peers

OUTLINE

Use this outline as you read the chapter. Enter your questions, comments, and notes in the space provided. Write down terms or statements you don't understand, with their page numbers.

THEORIES OF SOCIALIZATION

Evolutionary Approaches

Environmental/Learning Approaches

Cognitive-Developmental Approaches

Sociocultural Approaches

SOCIALIZATION WITHIN THE FAMILY

Parenting Styles

Classics of Research
Parenting Styles: The Work of Diana Baumrind

Ethnic and Cultural Factors

The Role of Fathers

The Child's Contribution

THE FAMILY AS A SYSTEM

Siblings

Grandparents and Other Family Members

Divorce

Alternative Family Composition

SOCIALIZATION BY PEERS

Typical Peer Relations

Cognitive Contributions

Processes of Peer Influence

VARIATIONS IN PEER RELATIONS

Friendship

Popularity and Problems

Applications
Interventions to Help Children with Problems

FAMILY AND PEERS

Siblings and Peers

Parents and Peers

On the Cutting Edge
Peer Relations as a Source of Resilience

Learning Objectives

Upon completion of Chapter 16 you should be able to discuss the following topics. Check off those you are confident that you can discuss well. Re-read the material in the text for the topics about which you are less confident. Record the important points from your reading in the space below each topic.

1. Discuss the notion proposed by evolutionary psychologists that many social behaviors, including parental caregiving and behaviors towards peers, have a biological basis.

2. Discuss how parents and peers can affect children's behavior and development from the social-learning perspective.

3. Discuss how interactions with parents and peers promote moral development and cognitive development in children according to the cognitive-developmental approach.

4. Discuss how the sociocultural approach views the role of parents and peers in socialization.

5. Describe the dimensions of *parental warmth* and *parental control*.

6. Identify and differentiate between the four styles of parenting identified by Diana Baumrind. Explain how parental warmth and parental control combine to yield these four styles.

7. Explain how styles of parenting may be influenced by ethnic and cultural differences.

8. Discuss how fathers compare with mothers in terms of caregiving and parenting roles.

9.   Explain how characteristics of the child can influence parental behavior.

10.   Describe how relationships with siblings, including sibling rivalry, develop with age. How do sibling relationships affect development?

11.   Discuss the roles that grandparents play in children's development.

12.   Describe the short-term and longer-term effects of divorce. What factors appear to determine these effects?

13.   Discuss risks and benefits associated with adoption.

14.   Discuss what is currently known about children of gay and lesbian parents.

15.   Describe the nature of interactions with peers in infancy.

16.   Compare and contrast two systems for classifying the play of preschoolers (i.e., according to cognitive level and according to social level).

17.   Discuss the importance and influence of the peer group in later childhood.

18.   Describe the findings of the Robbers Cave Experiment.

19.   Discuss how social-cognitive abilities, such as social problem-solving skills, may be important to the development of peer relations.

20.   Discuss the role of peers as models and as agents of reinforcement and punishment..

21.   Discuss the relative influences of peers and parents on children's behaviors, attitudes, and choices.

22.   Describe how older and younger children differ in their conceptions of friendship.

23.   Discuss how similarity influences children's selection of friends.

24.   Briefly describe the aspects of interaction that differentiate children who become friends from those who do not, according to John Gottman's research.

25.   Compare and contrast children's behavior with friends and non-friends, in terms of prosocial behaviors, conflict and its resolution, and intimacy.

26.   Discuss how friendship can be beneficial for children's self-esteem and social support.

27. Compare three types of sociometric techniques. Do sociometric measures yield a valid picture of a child's social standing?

28. Describe the indirect and the behavioral correlates of popularity in children.

29. Contrast *rejected, neglected,* and *controversial* children. How do these children differ? Will they outgrow their problems?

30. Describe several intervention approaches that have been used to help children with problems in peer relations.

31. Discuss how culture may influence the relationship between aggression and shyness and sociometric status.

32. Compare and contrast children's sibling relationships with their peer relationships.

33. Discuss how security of attachment in infancy is related to later peer relationships.

34. Outline four ways that Ladd has described in which parents can serve as managers, influencing the frequency and nature of their children's peer interactions.

35.   Discuss how parental discipline methods are related to children's peer relationships.

36.   Describe four ways in which positive peer relations can serve as protective factors against family adversity.

KEY TERMS

Parental warmth _____

_____

Parental control _____

_____

Parenting style _____

_____

Authoritative parenting _____

_____

Authoritarian parenting _____

_____

Permissive parenting _____

_____

Uninvolved (disengaged) parenting _____

_____

Sibling rivalry _____

_____

Extended family ______________________________

____

Blended family ______________________________

____

Pretend play ______________________________

____

Parallel play ______________________________

____

Group ______________________________

____

Clique ______________________________

____

Social problem-solving skills ______________________________

____

Friendship ______________________________

____

Behavioral homophyly ______________________________

____

Social support ______________________________

____

Sociometric techniques ______________________________

____

Rejected child _____

_____

Neglected child _____

_____

Controversial child _____

_____

Social withdrawal _____

_____

Peer-mediated intervention _____

_____

Resilient children _____

_____

FILL-IN EXERCISES

Fill in the word or words that best fit in the spaces below.

1.   According to social learning theory, both parents and peers affect a child's behavior through _____ and _____ behavior, and through _____ learning that results from exposure to models .

2.   To Piaget, children's relations with adults are characterized by an imbalance of power, in which adults are in authority, whereas their relationship with peers is much more one of _____.

3.   Parents who are low in warmth, but high in control, are referred to as _____, whereas those who are high in both warmth and control are labeled _____. Those who are high in warmth, but low in control are referred to as _____, while those who are low in both warmth and control have been called _____.

4.   Children who are impulsive, immature, and disobedient may have been raised by _____ parents.

5.   Competitive feelings between two or more siblings are referred to as _____ _____.

6.   The term _____ family refers to a family unit that consists not only of parents and children, but also of at least one and sometimes several other adult relatives.

7.   The negative consequences of divorce appear greater for _____ *(boys/girls)* than for _____ *(boys/girls)*.

8.   A _____ family refers to a new family unit, resulting from remarriage, that consists of parents and children from previously separate families.

9.   Infants' initial interactions with peers are characterized as _____-centered.

10.   Play that involves using an object or person to symbolize something else is described as _____ play.

11.   A form of play in which children play next to each other and with similar materials, but with no real cooperation, is referred to as _____ play.

12.   The term _____ refers to a collection of children who interact regularly in a consistent, structured fashion and who share values and a sense of belonging. Some adolescents belong to a collection called a _____, consisting of 5 to 10 members whose shared interests and behavior patterns set them apart from their peers.

13.   The skills needed to resolve social dilemmas are referred to as social _____-_____ skills.

14.   Recent studies have shown simple forms of peer imitation in toddlers as young as _____ to _____ months.

15.   Although even young children realize the importance of mutual liking between friends, it is only in late childhood or adolescence that qualities such as _____ and _____ become central to children's thinking about friendship.

16.   One general factor central to most friendships is _____. The most important aspect of this factor focuses on behaviors and interests, and is referred to by psychologists as behavioral _____.

17.   Perhaps the most general benefit of friendship is that it provides _____ _____ -- resources provided by other people in times of uncertainty or stress.

18.   The sociometric technique in which children are asked "Tell me the names of three kids in the class you especially like" is referred to as the _____ technique.

19.   Three sets of social skills are especially important for popularity; popular children are skilled at _____ interaction with other children, _____ interaction, and at _____ conflict.

20.   A child who receives both many positive and many negative sociometric nominations is referred to as _____.

21.   The most consistent correlate of peer rejection is _____.

22.   Neglected children are often perceived by their peers as being _____. In China, children who display such behavior are more likely to be _____ *(below/above)* average in popularity.

23.   Self-imposed isolation from the peer group is referred to as _____ _____.

24.   In addition to training in social skills, rejected children have been helped through training in _____ skills, perhaps as a result of the subsequent improvement in their self-concept and general classroom behavior.

25.   The home lives of children with peer relations problems may be characterized by parents' use of _____ _____ as a discipline technique.

26.   Children who adapt positively and develop well, despite early environmental adversity are described as _____ children.

APPLICATION

Situation

Suppose you were to design an intervention program for rejected children. The intent of the program would be to teach the participants skills that would enable them to interact better with their peers, with the goal being to improve their acceptance in the peer group.

Questions to answer

1.   How would you initially identify the rejected children to participate in the intervention program?

2.   Based on what you've read in the chapter, what sorts of skills would be important to teach the children?

3.   What sorts of approaches would you employ to teach these skills?

4.   How could you determine whether your intervention had been successful? What sort of research design would you use (look back to Chapter 2 to refresh your memory)?

USING WHAT YOU HAVE LEARNED

Having just completed a course in child development, you find that your friends are always consulting you concerning issues related to children and families they know. This week is no exception. A friend asks to talk with you about a family she knows that is just going through a divorce. She has questions about the following issues. Based on what you've read, what would you say?

1. Does divorce affect kids?

2. Will the effects "wear off" soon, or are there long-lasting effects on children?

3. What kinds of changes in children's lives after the divorce may be important in terms of how children react?

4. The children will be living with their mom. Is contact with their dad important?

5. If their mom remarries, what issues might they expect in their new, "blended" family? Might there be differences in how the boys react, compared to the girls? What if their dad remarries?

6. Could their relationship with their grandparents be important in helping them adjust? How?

7. Could their relationships with friends be important in adjusting to the divorce? How

SAMPLE TEST QUESTIONS

1. According to Piaget's theory, interaction with peers is important as it leads to the ability to consider different perspectives, resulting in:

    a. moral realism
    b. moral relativism
    c. moral dilemma
    d. moral comparison

2. Parents who are loving and emotionally sensitive, but set few limits on behavior and provide little in the way of structure or predictability, are described as:

    a. authoritarian
    b. permissive
    c. uninvolved
    d. authoritative

3. Deborah developed an insecure attachment to her parents as an infant. As a child she showed low social competence and did poorly in school. As an adolescent, she has been frequently in trouble with the law and uses drugs a lot. In terms of parenting style, her parents likely:

    a. set few limits and provide little by way of attention or support
    b. are very demanding and enforce their demands with threats and punishment
    c. are caring and sensitive, and maintain a predictable environment
    d. set few limits, but provide encouragement and support

4. Studies examining father-infant attachment show that:

    a. infants rarely develop an attachment relationship with their fathers
    b. attachment can be as great with the father as with the mother
    c. even when father and baby have a very secure relationship, it is probably not at strong as the baby's relationship with the mother
    d. all of the above

5. Which of the following is true concerning siblings?

    a. Because temperaments are heritable, most siblings have similar temperaments.
    b. Siblings with difficult temperaments tend to get along best if both share this temperament.
    c. Siblings typically get along best when they have similar temperaments.
    d. All of the above

6. A family unit that consists not only of parents and children, but also of at least one and sometimes several other relatives is called a(n):

    a. blended family
    b. mixed family
    c. unconventional
    d. extended family

7. Which of the following is true concerning the effects of divorce?

   a. The effects are most evident in the time period immediately following the divorce.
   b. The effects of divorce generally dissipate with time and disappear by adolescence.
   c. Girls are more likely to react to divorce with increased aggression and defiant behavior.
   d. All of the above.

8. Infants as young as _____ look at, smile at, and touch other infants.

   a. 1 month
   b. 3 months
   c. 4 months
   d. 6 months

9. Children younger than grade-school age rarely engage in:

   a. functional play
   b. constructive play
   c. games with rules
   d. pretend play

10. Two-year-old Janey loves to bang her building blocks together, over and over again. This type of play is best categorized as

    a. functional play
    b. constructive play
    c. pretend play
    d. games with rules

11. Manal and Linda are playing beside one another at the sandbox, using the same toys, but are not really playing together. What type of play is this?

    a. cooperative play
    b. parallel play
    c. solitary play
    d. associative play

12. In preschool-aged children, imitating peers is generally:

    a. regarded negatively, as it is viewed as making fun of others
    b. unlikely to occur as it requires more advanced cognitive abilities
    c. responded to positively
    d. largely ignored by other children

13.   Which of the following is **NOT** true about relationships between friends?

    a.   conflict occurs less often among friends than among non-friends
    b.   children share more with friends than with non-friends
    c.   children are more likely to engage in self-disclosure with friends than with non-friends
    d.   all of the above **ARE** true about relationships with friends

14.   Which of the following are categories of children's social supports?

    a.   informational support   b.   instrumental support
    c.   emotional support   d.   all of the above

15.   Which technique for measuring popularity involves naming some specific number of well-liked peers?

    a.   paired-comparison technique
    b.   rating-scale technique
    c.   nomination technique
    d.   sociometric technique

16.   The principal difference between rejected and neglected children is that:

    a.   although both receive few positive nominations, rejected children also receive few negative nominations
    b.   although both receive few positive nominations, neglected children also receive few negative nominations
    c.   although both receive few negative nominations, rejected children also receive few positive nominations
    d.   although both receive few negative nominations, neglected children also receive few positive nominations

17.   Which of the following describes the behavior of neglected children?

    a.   disruptive behavior
    b.   overly intrusive attempts to enter groups
    c.   fewer and more hesitant attempts to enter groups
    d.   antisocial, inappropriate behavior

18.   Which of the following techniques have been found to be effective interventions with children with peer relationship problems?

    a.   teaching perspective-taking skills
    b.   training in social problem-solving abilities
    c.   training in academic skills
    d.   all of the above

19.   Longitudinal studies indicate that:

   a.   children almost always outgrow their peer relationship problems
   b.   compared to neglect, peer rejection is not very stable over time
   c.   neglected children are at risk for later juvenile delinquency
   d.   rejected children are at risk for problems later in life

20.   Ladd identified four roles parents may play in influencing the frequency and nature of their children's peer interactions. According to Ladd, parents may serve as:

   a.   designers, mediators, supervisors, consultants
   b.   reinforcers, punishers, mediators, supervisors
   c.   discipline agents, mediators, supervisors, consultants
   d.   providers of social support, attachment-figures, caregivers, nurturers

ANSWERS

FILL-IN EXERCISES

1. reinforcing, punishing; observational   2. equals   3. authoritarian; authoritative; permissive; uninvolved (disengaged)   4. permissive   5. sibling rivalry   6. extended   7. boys; girls   8. blended
9. object   10. pretend   11. parallel   12. group; clique   13. problem-solving   14. fifteen, twenty
15. loyalty, intimacy   16. similarity; homophyly   17. social support   18. nomination   19. initiating; maintaining; resolving   20. controversial   21. aggression   22. shy; above   23. social withdrawal
24. academic   25. power assertion   26. resilient

SAMPLE TEST QUESTIONS

1. b	11. b
2. b	12. c
3. a	13. a
4. b	14. d
5. c	15. c
6. d	16. b
7. a	17. c
8. d	18. d
9. c	19. d
10. a	20. a